WALK THE LAKES

40 EASY WALKS
Selected and described by John Parker

John Bartholomew & Son Ltd
Edinburgh

British Library Cataloguing in Publication Data
Parker, John
    Walk the Lakes - (A Bartholomew map and guide)
    1. Lake District (England) - Description and travel - Guide-books
    I. Title
    914.27'804858   DA670.L1
    ISBN 0-7028-8111-2

First published in Scotland 1983
by John Bartholomew & Son Ltd.,
Duncan Street, Edinburgh EH9 1TA
Reprinted 1983, 1984, 1986

ISBN 0 7028 8111 2

Printed in Scotland
by John Bartholomew & Son Ltd.

CONTENTS

KEY MAP FOR THE WALKS

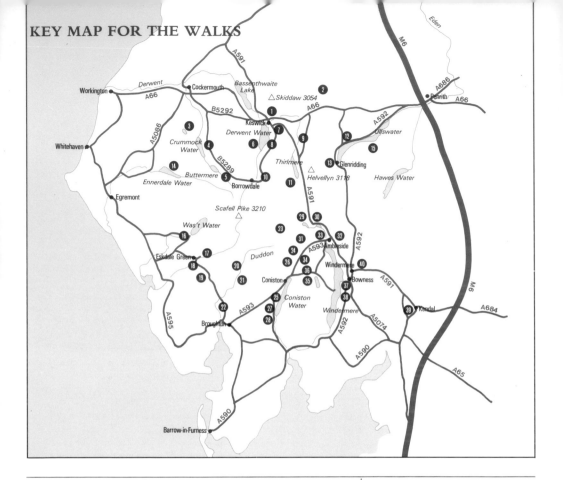

KEY TO SCALE AND MAP SYMBOLS

SCALE 1:63 360

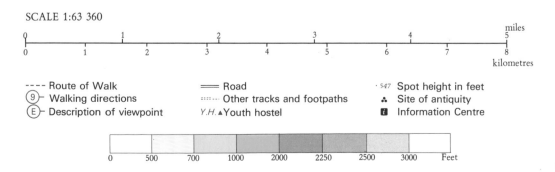

	Route of Walk		Road		Spot height in feet
(9)-	Walking directions	::::	Other tracks and footpaths	♣	Site of antiquity
(E)-	Description of viewpoint	Y.H.▲	Youth hostel	🛈	Information Centre

4

1 ON THE REAL ART OF WALKING

Some walkers revel in mileage; some 'collect' long-distance footpaths like other people collect stamps while others run around many miles in wild country on map-reading races. Some would point to the need of modern spoon-fed society to tax sloppy muscles once in a while. But is there not also another, perhaps greater, need ? True recreation is a re-creation. In the natural beauty of the countryside one can find an oasis of reassurance in that confusing desert of changing modern values. It is a 'going-back' to the beginning. The true art of walking consists not of packing distance into moments, but packing enjoyable moments into distance.

Who would enjoy old wine by gulping draughts of it? It must be held on the palate and savoured slowly. Many perhaps could easily 'knock off' four of the walks described here in one day. That would be foolish when there is so much to savour in each one. What this book does, is point to a few features on these selected walks and leave the rest for discovery. What is left to the walker is his or her awareness.

It must be recognised however that in the normal human state awareness is dulled. Overwhelmed by the sensations pouring in at us from all side we habitually filter them out and accept only what we want and think we need. We receive only what we are 'tuned in' to receive. It could be as our own Lake District bard, William Wordsworth said:

'The world is too much with us; late and soon,
Getting and spending we lay waste our powers:
Little we see in Nature that is ours;
We have given our hearts away, ...' (1).

But all is not lost if we realise that these limitations are self-inflicted. All we have to do is to awaken our senses and willingly accept nature's messages in sight, scent and sound. That means complete relaxation in freedom. There is no need to accept the tyranny of a distance walking programme; no need to look on the Lake District as some vast open air gymnasium. Distance and muscle straining is not the objective here. What we look for in these walks is not quantity, but quality.

'Ah', some might say, 'but the best views are from the mountain tops'. That is nonsense. The best views surely consist of the two extreme elements juxtaposed; the active and the passive. Mountains and lake, or the frozen violence of steep crags set above the green calm of the dale. It is true that John Ruskin (1819-1900), the supreme arbiter of good taste in scenery said 'Mountains are the beginning and the end of all natural scenery.' (2) He spent his last 25 years in contemplating them from the supreme low-level viewpoint of his Coniston lakeside house. A high viewpoint is not necessary; a low one is often just as good and indeed can be better.

The pleasures of these walks can be shared by any reasonably active family, which is why they were chosen. Beyond modest physical effort and a minimum of equipment, all that is needed is that 'eye to perceive, and a heart to enjoy'. (3).

References

(1) Wordsworth W. *The World is Too Much With Us. Miscellaneous Sonnets.* Part 1; XXX111.

(2) Ruskin J. *Modern Painters.* London, 1888. Vol IV; Part V: Chap 20.

(3) Wordsworth W. *Guide to the Lakes.* London 1835.

2 WHAT EQUIPMENT ?

For ordinary fell walking it is not necessary to purchase expensive equipment as though you were about to tackle the north face of the Eiger. It is bad logic to assume that, for instance, a pair of boots good enough for scaling the Alps must be good enough for Loughrigg Fell. Ice and snow are not the norm here. Footwear should be reasonably strong, not too heavy and preferably worn over wool socks or stockings. Nylon can give blisters. Soles of the boots should be cleated or wedged, rather than smooth. Sliding around wastes a lot of energy and can lead to falls and broken bones as easily as a fall of several feet. Boots should grip neatly and comfortably round the ankle so preventing the feet moving and rubbing into blisters. To summarise; boots should be strong, light, comfortable and provide grip.

Clothing too should be comfortable. As it can rain very hard in the Lake District it is advisable to carry a light rucksack with a light waterproof and if possible waterproof trousers too. These should protect you from the worst of the weather unless you are walking in the depths of winter, when more specialist clothing is likely to be necessary.

Carrying a rucksack leaves the hands and arms free. If walking as a family, the loads can be shared. It is always advisable to carry something to eat as walks can take longer than anticipated, especially if one lingers at a particularly pleasant viewpoint or quiet corner. A basic first aid kit with a few self-adhesive dressings for possible blisters and cuts, and an ointment for insect bites should be carried. In mid-summer it is a good idea to take along a proprietary brand of insect repellent.

An one inch to the mile (1:63360) map, as well as this guide book, is useful for putting the walk into context and for identifying the distant terrain.

3 PUBLIC RIGHTS OF WAY

There is more freedom to walk in the Lake District than possibly anywhere else in Britain. On offer there is everything, from easy walks by lake shores to rough scrambles on the high fells. The fells are open to all, not by right, but by traditional let. But it should be clear that though the Lake District is a National Park that does not mean that all the land belongs to the nation. Most of the land is privately owned, and farmed or grazed, and much of the valley land is enclosed. However, a vast network of public rights of way through this private land means that little is denied to the walker. With a map the rights of way can be identified; they are marked in red on the one inch (1:63360) map; public footpaths as red dots and bridleways as dashes.

The National Parks and Access to the Countryside Act 1949 tidied up the law on rights of way. Following the process of public consultation, maps were drawn by the County authorities of England and Wales showing all the rights of way. Copies of the definitive maps are available for public inspection. Once on the map the right of way becomes irrefutable.

What the right means

Any member of the public can pass freely on a public right of way, on foot, on a footpath, on horseback or cycle on a bridleway. No one can lawfully interfere with that right; not even the landowner. It would be wrong, for instance, for a landowner to move anyone away with the argument that the definitive map was wrongly drawn. It may be so, but until the error is lawfully corrected by the prescribed process the path remains a public thoroughfare.

The walker has the right to pass along the right of way and rest on it for a reasonable length of time. He has no right, for instance, to take a deck chair, a radio, and a picnic basket and sunbathe on it! The landowner or his tenant must not obstruct the right of passage in any way. He must maintain the stiles and gates on the path so as to offer unrestricted passage, a duty which seems rather unfair on him, though he can obtain help in meeting the maintenance cost from the Highways Authority. The landowner must not erect any notice which might discourage, or lead the public to believe that a right of way does not exist.

A member of the public has the right to remove any obstruction which he might encounter on the route.

He has, however, no right to go purposely onto a right of way, knowing it to be obstructed, with the intention of removing the obstruction. It is required that any report of a known obstruction should be communicated to the Highways Authority (in the case of the Lake District to the Lake District Special Planning Board, Busher Walk, Kendal) who can compel the owner to remove the obstruction, or can remove it and charge the landowner with the cost of doing so.

A walker can take his dog with him on a public right of way so long as it is under close control. A farmer has the right to shoot a dog which is worrying, or he has reason to suspect is about to worry, sheep. Under the Wildlife and Countryside Act 1982 it is even an offence to have a dog not under close control in a field containing sheep; the dog owner can be fined heavily. Under the same Act a farmer can put a mature bull into a field crossed by a right of way so long as it is a beef bull, which is usually more docile; cows must be present too. How the ordinary walker can tell one bull breed from another is not clear. If it is a black and white Friesian, which is a dairy bull, it is illegal and definitely to be avoided!

No one can drive any vehicle, including a motor-cycle, along a public footpath or bridleway unless he has the landowner's consent. It would be wrong to assume every motor cyclist on a public path is offending. Some shepherds now use motorcycles to get to, and to round up sheep.

The Highways Authority has the responsibility of maintaining rights of way, and the bridges on it, in reasonable condition. That does not mean, of course, that it should pave them all or do anything beyond ensuring that the users are not unduly impeded by extreme wear and tear. The Authority has the duty to place, with the consent of the Parish Councils concerned, footpath signs at the points where public rights of way leave public highways. However it could take many years, at the present rate of progress, before this duty is completed. The Authority can also waymark paths, and erect further sign posts on the route, if necessary.

The responsibilities

Rights usually carry responsibilities and these are a matter of reasonable commonsense. 'The rights of the individuals should be thus far limited' said John Stuart Mill, 'that he must not be a nuisance to other people'. If a walker must pass through a closed gate on his route, naturally he should close it behind him. If there is a group of walkers, the rule should be not more than two abreast across paths on farm fields, every square yard (metre) of grass is vital to the hill farmer.

4 A CODE FOR COUNTRYGOERS

No countrygoer should ever drop litter. Everyone knows this but it bears repeating for the National Park authority, and The National Trust, using hard-pressed staff and volunteers, have to make constant costly efforts to remove the mess left by unthinking people. The fact that a footpath is clean does not mean, alas, that all walkers are respecting the countryside. It could mean that a group of volunteers has just cleaned it. It is no trouble to pocket litter until it can be disposed of correctly.

Obviously flowers and plants encountered on a walk should not be taken but left for others passing to enjoy. To use the excuse 'I have only taken a few' is futile. If everyone only took a few the country would be devastated. If young wild animals are encountered they should be left well alone. For instance, although they might not often be seen in full daylight, deer, both roe and red, are common in the Lake District. If a fawn or a deer calf is discovered lying still in the grass it would be wrong to assume that it has been abandoned. Mothers hide their offspring while they go away to graze and browse and return to them at feeding time. If the animals are touched it could mean that they will be abandoned as the human scent might deter the mother from returning to her offspring. Similarly with baby birds, who have not yet mastered flight; they may appear to have been abandoned but often are being watched by their parents who might be waiting for a walker to pass on before coming out to give flight lesson two!

What appear to be harmful snakes should not be killed because firstly the 'snake' could be a slow worm, which looks like a snake but is really a harmless legless lizard, and second, even if it were an adder (they are quite common) it will escape if given the opportunity. Adders are part of the pattern of nature and should not be persecuted. They rarely bite unless they are handled; a foolish act, which is not uncommon; or stood on, which is rare, as the snakes are usually basking in full view and are very quick to escape. Adder bites are rarely serious and panic is quite unnecessary.

For his or her own safety a walker should take care when walking on country roads. The advice usually given is to walk on the right so as to face oncoming traffic, but sometimes this can be dangerous. The rule should be qualified with the advice that the outside should be taken on blind bends so that traffic in both directions can see the walker.

Countrygoers should take care not to start fires. The danger time in the Lake District is usually in a dry spring when the previous year's bracken and undergrowth is tinder dry. A carelessly discarded cigarette end can cause thousands of pounds worth of damage.

Lastly, remote homes and communities depend on fell side becks and pools for their water supplies, even when the Water Authority's huge extraction plants are close at hand. Everyone should be quite sure before bathing that the tempting pools or becks are not someone's supply. Ask first!

When walking over enclosed land it is necessary to read your map accurately so as to avoid trespassing and damage to walls by crossing at the wrong place; a frequent cause for complaint. The stiles and gates provided should *always* be used.

5 MAP READING

A map is a representation, on flat paper, of the three-dimensional features of the earth. Some boast that given an one inch to the mile (1:63360) map of some strange country they can scan a part of it, and have a mental picture of the landscape it represents. This is possibly an exaggeration. The map certainly details the bones of the landscape; the flesh is left to the imagination. As a map has severe spatial and dimensional limitations it is necessary to interpret. This needs practice. Usually a family walking party has one good map reader and that task is left to him or her. This is unwise; everyone should have a turn! Map reading is important as it is the key to enjoying the countryside. Anyone who lacks this easily acquired skill is denied an essential freedom.

The map's key and the scale are detailed at its base. A brief study is necessary. Once the key features of roads, footpaths, watercourses and hills have been learned you should not get lost. One of the most common mistakes to make when map reading is the wrong identification of the point where you are standing. The path or road is identifiable but the precise place is not. The problem can be solved by correct orientation of the map; that is place the map so that the top is towards the north. The easiest way to do this is to place a compass on it with the north point on the compass card pointing to the top. The map, compass card and the map reader (if he is to avoid reading it sideways or upside down) should all be turned until the compass needle points to magnetic north, which is currently eight degrees to the west of north (352 degrees on the scale). Once the map is orientated, some of the visible physical features can be identified and then with the aid of the map your position in relation to them fixed. Another way to orientate a map without a compass is to turn it until some identifiable feature in the landscape (*eg* a church) is lined up with the map, then all the other features should fit into place.

Orientation is particularly useful at a viewpoint when you are trying to identify distant features, such as hills or mountain peaks.

Excusably, one can regard the need to watch the time as a tyranny when walking for pleasure. However a watch is also a useful tool when map reading. For example, if you knew that it was 1100hrs when you were standing at the tarn and you know that your family walks about two miles (3km) per hour on a reasonably level route and that it is now 1130hrs, then on the one inch to the mile (1:63360) map you should fix yourself about inch (2.5cm) from the tarn. This, of course assumes level ground. The other features on the map which one must master, are the contours. Experience might prove that you need to take account in your calculations of the need to add five minutes to every 100 feet (30.5m) of climbing, which is fairly average for a family. So if the journey from the tarn involved a 100 feet (30.5m) of climb as you see it from the interpretation of the contours and a glance back at the terrain, that takes five minutes ($^1/_6$ in/4mm) off your distance on the map.

With this formula you can estimate the time it will take to do one of the walks in this book, but to the walking time one has to add talking time, not to mention the looking, photographing, the eating, the sunbathing, and the luxurious idleness time. All this might be something of a challenge to map readers, but the exercise can be entertaining and the experience in the long run invaluable! However, good map reading still requires lots of practice.

6 SOME PRECAUTIONARY NOTES - SAFETY

The walks in this book have been chosen with safety as well as enjoyment in mind. However accidents can happen even in the easiest terrain and 90 per cent of these can be avoided. There are the obvious precautions of keeping children away from quarry and rock faces, holes and unstable river banks. The falls which happen are usually caused by poor, particularly smooth-soled, footwear. What might be suitable for the town is a liability in the country. A fall can also be caused by the bad placing of feet, almost always *on the descent.* This usually happens when someone is in a hurry or is losing concentration from tiredness. Boisterous children must be restrained from running downhill. It is absolutely vital to look at where you are about to place your feet. Remember dry steep grass, or wet grass, can be as slippy as the other more obvious hazard of smooth wet rock. Tripping is another cause of falls. Watchfulness is again the answer. Accident records for walkers in the Lake District show a surprising number which have been caused by tripping over a dog lead!

Bogs in the vicinity of these walks are not generally considered to be a danger, but can cause some discomfort! Beware of ground which is bright green, or grey-green with sphagnum moss. If you find yourself bogged down, make for the bracken or heather, neither of which can grow on bog.

Even the most careful can sometimes sprain an ankle. Should an accident happen to a member of the family and you are near enough the road to help yourself, then you or someone else should try to get to a telephone. Dial 999 and ask for 'Police' and 'Mountain rescue'; give accurate details of location and, if possible, the injury. That is all that is necessary at that stage. If it is your practice to walk alone, then the most obvious precaution for you to take is to leave route details with someone at 'base'. This seems elementary, but there have been many occasions on which someone has not returned from a walk and no one else has any idea where that person intended to go. A search party has then to rely on guesswork; that could mean many expensive man-hours, or days before the casualty is found. If you leave the details, a search party has a better idea, at least, of where to look.

Lastly, safety of property; some of these walks start from quiet unobserved areas where thieves can be undisturbed. It is not a good idea to leave the car unlocked or valuables on display in it. Lock everything in the boot.

7 THE NATIONAL PARK AND THE NATIONAL TRUST

The Lake District was already attracting great numbers of tourists before Wordsworth wrote his famous *Guide to the Lakes* in the first half of last century, and the wealthy were also buying tracts of prime scenic countryside on which to build their own country seats. Wordsworth in his Guide's concluding chapter expresses a hope that 'better taste should prevail' and adds: 'In this wish the author will be joined by persons of pure taste throughout the whole island, who, by their visits (often repeated) to the Lakes in the North of England, testify that they deem the district a sort of national property, in which every man has a right and interest who has an eye to perceive and a heart to enjoy'. Since that time there have been changes that Wordsworth would have deplored, but his 'wish' has received a good deal of sympathetic, if somewhat tardy, response. The world's first National Park was born at Yellowstone in the United States in 1872. The first practical moves in conservation in Britain came much later and took a rather different, perhaps typically British, shape.

The National Trust

Late in the 19th century the incumbent at Crosthwaite church in Keswick was one Canon Hardwicke Rawnsley, an extraordinarily energetic man; poet, traveller, athlete, historian, preacher and campaigner, as well as passionate lover of the Lake District. In 1890 a parishioner told him that he had been compelled to buy some land from his neighbour to prevent his felling some fine trees. Rawnsley accepted the idea that the purchase of property was the only sure way to preserve it, and he was concerned about the growing threats to unspoilt country and historical sites. With the supporting efforts of another great campaigner and reformer, Octavia Hill and another friend, Robert Hunter, Solicitor to the Post Office, an organisation was founded which sought to acquire and preserve property, by gift or purchase by public subscription. It was thus that The National Trust, a charity, was officially launched in 1895.

Some of the Trust's first acquisitions were in Rawnsley's own area. In 1902 Brandelhow, on the west side of Derwentwater, was bought by public subscription. Nearby Manesty Park was bought in 1908 before it could be parcelled up into building plots. Over the years since large areas of the Lake District have come into the care of The National Trust. Notable benefactors have included Dr George Trevelyan, the historian who gave properties in Langdale, and artist/author Beatrix Potter, who as a girl had met Canon Rawnsley. Thanks to her the Trust gained some 4000 acres (1620 ha) and 14 farms. Now The National Trust is the largest landowner in the Lake District and has made it possible for traditional farming to continue in many dales, and vast areas of broadleaf woodlands to be protected.

The National Park

The Lake District National Park is the largest of the National Parks in England and Wales, with 866 square miles (2242 sq km). The Act which established National Parks came into being 140 years after Wordsworth's expressions of concern, and 77 years after Yellowstone. The first strongly organised pressure for National Parks and access to mountains came during the 1920s and '30s when walking and mountaineering became popular pastimes and access to open country in some parts of Britain was much restricted. The outbreak of war postponed progress, and following the reports of John Dower on the need, and the Hobhouse Committee's recommendations on implementation, an Act, The National Parks and Access to the Countryside Act 1949, was passed. 'People need the refreshment which is obtainable from the beauty and quietness of unspoilt country'. The provision for those needs of the people, and the protection from spoilation, were written into the Act.

In many countries of the world National Parks are areas of wilderness hardly influenced by man, and the land of these parks is owned by the nation or state. There is no true wilderness left in Britain. The 'natural' beauty of the landscape reflects the pattern of husbandry, and with so many owning and making a living from the land nationalisation of it was not contemplated. A British National Park is a defined area of unspoilt countryside, usually with some wild, if not wilderness, country, which is specially protected from unsuitable development; public access for its en-joyment is secured, and due regard made for the needs of the local community.

The National Park authority must exercise planning control, but must also provide information and ranger services. In the Lake District the authority also owns a visitor centre at Brockhole, Windermere, and has responsibility for the maintenance of public footpaths and bridleways. It also owns extensive areas of hill commonland, woodland and lake.

The National Trust, the charity, and the National Park, the local government authority, work closely with other large landowners, the Forestry Commission and the Water Authority, to provide protected public access unrivalled anywhere else in Britain. It is indeed as Wordsworth said 'a sort of national property' for those 'with eyes to perceive and hearts to enjoy'

Addresses

The National Trust
National Trust Regional Office,
Rothay Holme, Rothay Road,
Ambleside, Cumbria LA22 OEJ

The Lake District National Park
The Lake District Special Planning Board,
Busher Walk, Kendal, Cumbria

8 THE GEOLOGY OF THE LAKE DISTRICT

Nothing seems more permanent than mountains. But the shapes of the Lake District mountains tells of cataclysmal earth movements and violent upheavals. But all in the millions of years past? The enormity of geological time is extremely difficult to comprehend. The human life span is a cursory second of time in the infinite. But in the great timescale the mountains still move. The rocks are eroded by weather and are drawn down by gravity to the valleys. During rapid temperature changes you can see it happening on Wastwater Screes. On the other hand it is possible that the great granite mass which underlies much of the Lake District could be very gradually pushing upwards. The scenery is not static. It is dynamic.

The history of the Lake District over the last 530 million years can be seen in the landscape at the present time. The interpretation of some details has often caused some controversy, but there is general agreement on the major events.

The oldest rocks are the *Skiddaw Slates.* These were formed from sediments of gravel, grit and mud laid down in a shallow sea and later subjected to great pressure. Their age is usually put into the Ordovician period; some 530 million years ago. Most of this rock series now resembles shale rather than slate. It is minutely jointed and with the action of weather and frost has broken down into small flakes.

After the deposition of the Skiddaw Slates came several millions of years of volcanic action. Lava burst out from below the surface and flowed over the landscape. Explosions threw out hot 'bombs' of rock. Ash settled to huge depths. All this mass of varied material settled to a depth of up to two miles (3km) and formed what are known as the *Borrowdale Volcanic* series of rocks.

After that the whole area was covered by a shallow sea, and erosion material, at first calcareous, then huge amounts of grit and mud settled in layers to a depth of two and a half miles (4km). This was in the Silurian period between 440 and 410 million years ago.

It can be imagined that the then lakeless Lake District consisted of three very thick layers of material each on top of the other. During the Devonian period the earth's crust was subject to much movement. The area was thrust upwards into a dome. Each of the rock types reacted differently according to the position of the centre of the thrust. Once the upper layers were fractured, for instance, the more malleable Skiddaw Slate beneath was pushed through to a great height, then hot sandstorms and heavy rains wore down the upper layers. Much of Skiddaw Slates' topmost parts, and a substantial area of the Silurian rocks were swept away. In the central parts the much harder Borrowdale Volcanics were left exposed. Therefore the Skiddaw Slates were left uppermost in the north, the Volcanics in the centre, and the Silurian to the south.

From 345 to 280 million years ago there followed the Carboniferous period. The area was again covered by a sea rich in life. The central part of the district probably remained as an island. The deposits in this sea formed the carboniferous limestone. Subsequently much of this was swept away leaving a rim around the Lake District. The Permo Trias period followed; the area became hot and arid. The desert sands of this time were later solidified into the New Red Sandstone, which again was mainly swept away from the central dome.

The tertiary period, 65 million years ago brought new upheavals to the planet. This 'Alpine' movement produced the Alps, the Himalayas and the Andes. Again the Lake District's dome was raised high. Fracture lines appeared, in general radiating from the centre, but varying in direction according to the reaction of the material. These formed the basis of the valley patterns we know today.

The next great catastrophe was nearer our own time. About one a half million years ago the climate changed dramatically and the whole of the northern hemisphere was covered in ice. The subsequent movement and melting of the ice hollowed out the valleys and lake beds, and swept away vegetation. The heavy rainstorms later moved any remaining loose material. Thus the dales were sculpted and the lakes were formed.

The visible history

What is seen now still reads historically from north to south. The mountains and hills of *Skiddaw Slates* which lie in a curving band, from the north to the west, are covered by carboniferous and sandstones nearer the coast, and reappear to the south-west at Black Combe. Because much of this material is shaley and craggy outcrops seldom occur. The fells have angular outlines. Typically of course there is Skiddaw itself (3054ft/930.8m) with its neighbour Saddleback (2847ft/867.7m). The fells to the west of Derwentwater, Causey Pike and Grisedale Pike, are of the same material, and the rock is also very evident in the fells on the east side of Buttermere, to the north and west around Crummock Water and Loweswater as well as the northern end of Ennerdale Water. There is good soil depth on these rock forms which allows trees and heather to grow naturally.

In the central Lake District roughly north-east to south-west are the high craggy fells of the *Borrowdale Volcanics.* The soaring walls of the Scafells, Great Gable, the Borrowdale fells, as well as Coniston Old Man in the south-west through the Langdales and Bowfell; and eastwards through Helvellyn to High Street; these are all examples of Borrowdale Volcanics. They excite the interest of rock-climbers and mountaineers. As the iron-hard rock does not break down easily the minerals are 'locked in' and the shallow acidic soils do not support a rich vegetation. The alpine plants are found mainly where springs leach the minerals to the surface. The deeper soils are often covered in bracken, very beautifully coloured in autumn, but useless to the hill farmers' sheep. From the hard 'tuff' in this series of rocks Neolithic settlers hammered out stone axes and exported them to many parts of Britain. From another type of rock, formed from fine volcanic sediments in water, come the famous green-slate, still quarried and much in demand for its wearing and decorative qualities. It is used for the facings of prestigious buildings.

The *Silurian* rock types are visible in the south of the Lake District. These soft slates and mudstones produce an acid soil in which trees and forests find root and regenerate quite readily. The typical scenery, much in evidence around Windermere, consists of rounded hills, often with a good deal of tree cover. The Forestry Commission's largest forest, at Grizedale is also in this area.

The *limestones* and the *sandstones* are round the fringe of the district. There are several exposures of granite. *Granites* are *Plutons,* formed from Volcanic material cooling slowly beneath the earth's crust. The Lake District granites were probably formed during the Devonian earth movements when cavities and fractures in the rocks became filled with the super-heated magma thrust up from the depths of the earth. The granites were uncovered by later erosion and notably these can be seen at Shap in the north-east, or on the north end of the Helvellyn range near Threlkeld. There are also exposures of granite types in Eskdale, Wasdale, and Ennerdale to the west. These Plutonic 'bubbles' are surrounded by rocks much changed by the tremendous heat; metamorphic. The zone between is known as the 'metamorphic aureole'. The cracks in the metamorphic rocks were sometimes filled with molten minerals and here are found the metals notable in the Lake District, iron, copper and lead. The metals were mined from Roman times until early this century. The more productive mines were in the Newlands Valley and the western side of Derwentwater, and at Greenside, above Glenridding on the side of Helvellyn.

The last effect on the landscape was man made. Before there was substantial human settlement the whole area was covered in forest. This has been removed over a period of four thousand years. Much of it was destroyed from early Elizabethan times up to the last century to provide charcoal for the hungry iron furnaces. The increase in sheep grazing has meant that regeneration has been impossible. Much of the woodland and forest we now see was planted within the last century and a half. The lack of tree cover in many places has accelerated erosion and impoverished the soil.

LATRIGG

6½ miles (10.5km) 950ft (289.5m) Strenuous

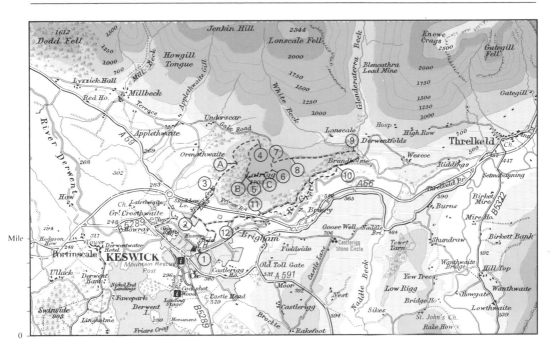

Visitors to Keswick, while naturally being attracted to the walk to Derwentwater cannot but be impressed by and may indeed want to climb the steep hill, crowned by struggling pines, on the north-east of the town. The heights give spectacular views. A direct ascent looks an eye-popping, heart-thumper, but there is an easy way which takes a more civilised zig-zag. The walk should be done in clear weather so that the view is seen at its glorious best. A walker should carry the full one inch to the mile (1:63360) map to identify the fells, nearly of all of which can be seen. Strong boots with good cleated or wedged soles are essential.

1 *The walk starts at Keswick. Take the road which goes past Fitz Park and the museum and loops round the old station site.*

2 *Take the lane opposite the estate which runs straight up between fences and hedges to cross the A66 by bridge.*

3 *Join path and continue on.*

A *A view here over Bassenthwaite and up to Skiddaw.*

4 *Before reaching the roadway ahead take sharp zig-zag right. Path continues to summit. Wet patches can be avoided with care.*

B *The magnificent view opens below and south. Derwentwater in its entirety and the tree clad Borrowdale. All the high fells can be*

identified including Scafell Pike and Scafell, Great Gable and Bowfell and Helvellyn. There is pleasant turf to sit on to enjoy it at leisure.

5 *Go left from summit.*

C *View of Saddleback ahead.*

6 *Cross stile and go left to follow fence.*

7 *At fence corner turn right to follow fence.*

8 *Join track and continue right.*

9 *Turn right and follow the tarmacadam lane.*

10 *Follow this lane on or take alternative, though rougher, route on the permitted path through wood.*

11 *Cross bridge over A66.*

12 *Follow lane on to T-junction then left to starting point.*

13

SOUTHER FELL

5 miles (8km) Moderate; wet areas; circuit

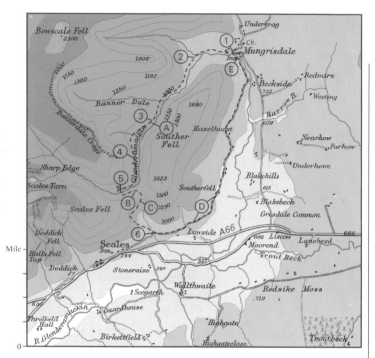

1 *Start at the Inn and bridge. Walk on until a lane is reached; a short distance on the left. Walk past the farm and on up an old mine track.*

2 *At the junction go left. The left-hand route is less clear on the ground.*

3 *Wet areas can be avoided with care by going upwards above them or down to the stony ground.*

A This is a pleasant secluded dale with a passive rather than dramatic aspect.

4 *Wet areas can be avoided with care.*

5 *Go down an angled path to a bridge and cross to a path going left on the far side of the river.*

B Good view down the valley and upwards to the northern end of Saddleback proper; the narrow ridge is known as 'Sharp Edge'.

C This is the summit of the path from which there is a view south to Helvellyn. If it is a clear day the central fells may be seen, with Scafell Pike, the highest point in England (3210ft/978m) to the south-west.

6 *Descend, avoiding the wet areas as far as possible, to the gate and on to a lane. Go left and follow the lane right through. If the gates are closed, open and then close them after you. The lane goes on to the Inn.*

D The rock here is *Skiddaw Slate*; really a sort of shale. Where water reaches the surface it leaches out minerals which provide a rich environment for a great variety of wild flowers to grow.

E The Inn was once a mill. The location could hardly have been better.

Souther is pronounced 'Sowter'. It is a spur off the mountain of Saddleback (otherwise Celtic 'Blencathra') and is unusual as it is almost completely surrounded by river; the Glenderamackin. Glenderamackin is another Celtic name; the area has Celtic connections, such as the nearby Carrock Fell where there are remains of a Celtic hill fort. It is said that a force of warriors haunts Souther Fell on Midsummer's Eve, but there has been no record of a sighting since the 18th century. At that time on several Midsummer Eves the column was led by mounted officers. With so much detail in the tales they may well be true!

The walk starts at the village of Mungrisdale. 'Grisdale', 'Grizedale' or 'Grisedale' abounds as a place name in the Lake District and this is Norse for 'dale of pigs'. Here the Celtic prefix 'Mung' ('Mungho' in another name) means 'dearest one'. It refers to the 7th century Celtic missionary St Kentigern to whom Mungrisdale's church is dedicated.

There is still a brooding Celtic mystery about the fell and the quiet circuit is an antidote to the noisy reality of the 20th century. Mungrisdale is reached from the A66 at a junction seven miles (11.3km) from Keswick and eight (12.9km) from Penrith.

14

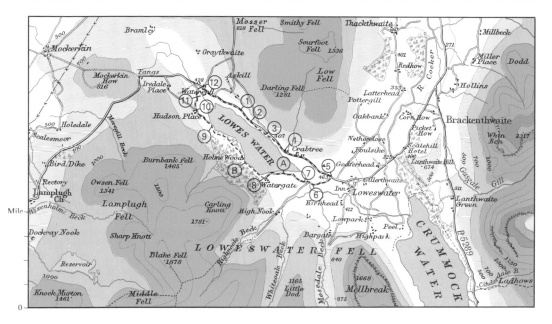

Loweswater is in the softer landscape of the Skiddaw Slate. The material is more properly described as a shale which breaks down to give a reasonable depth of soil. This means that much of the area not heavily grazed by stock is woodland. Lovely Loweswater, bordered by trees, is in the care of The National Trust. The lake is little more than a mile (1.6km) long and its circuit is an easy and pleasing stroll. Like most of the lakes, Loweswater probably takes its name from an ancient Norse owner; in this case Laghi; 'Laghi's Water'. The lake is unique in the Lake District in that its outflow flows in; that is the flow goes inwards (eastwards) towards the District's centre. It flows, in fact, into Crummock Water before

that lake flows outwards to the north as the River Cocker.

1 *Start the walk from a terraced lay-by to the north-east of the lake, between the road and the lake. Walk by the lake on the road.*

2 *Walk down and along the lake shore when possible.*

3 *If the water level is high you might have to walk on the road for a short distance.*

4 *Go left, back to the road, at a fence. Walk along the road.*

5 *Turn left and go down a tarmacadam lane.*

6 *After the curves in the road, watch for a gate on the right, for Watergate.*

7 *Go through the gate and along the track.*

A Viewpoint over the field to the lake.

8 *At Watergate, go through the gates and along the lakeside path.*

B Tree spotters can note the wide variety of hardwoods grown here. As this is National Trust land there is freedom to wander and identify species or to linger on the shore.

9 *Continue on the path alongside the wall and away from the lake.*

10 *Hudson Place. Turn right and go down a 'hollow lane'.*

11 *There is a choice of paths here. Go straight on, or turn right to cut the corner through a gate, over a slate bridge, then over a wooden bridge to the gate at the roadside.*

12 *Join the road and turn right to the starting point.*

15

CRUMMOCK WATER CIRCUIT

8½ miles (13.7 km) Strenuous; wet; rough

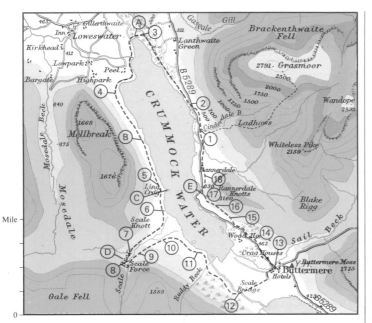

The glacial flow which ground out the valley north-westwards from the Central fells in the ice age left one large lake. Before the mountain sides were stabilised with herb and scrub the erosion of many storms created an alluvial plain in mid-lake splitting the water into what is now Buttermere at the head, and Crummock Water at the foot. Crummock is the larger lake with contrasting landscapes at both ends and is not without drama and beauty.

The walk around Crummock is away from the well-beaten tracks. It is, however, rough and wet underfoot. Waterproof boots, not wellington boots which might be too slippery, are recommended. With skill some of the boggy sections can be avoided. The walk includes some excellent viewpoints, and a look at Scale Force, a 130 foot (40m) waterfall, tucked aggravatingly in a narrow ravine which is not easy to reach.

1 *The walk starts at a car park on Cinderdale Common on the east side of Crummock Water. Walk north on the road side.*

2 *After a short distance, go over stile on the left and walk down to the lake shore. Follow the lakeshore path. There are several tracks converging onto a plainly seen path.*

3 *Take the left fork of the path round the foot of the lake, over bridges.*

A Excellent viewpoint of almost the full length of the lake. Rannerdale Knotts is the craggy point. The mountain on the left is Grasmoor.

4 *Join clearer path.*

B Fine shingle beaches. Look for the redness which betrays presence of iron. Ore was extracted in small quantities here in old times and was ferried across to the far shore where it was smelted in charcoal-fuelled hearths (Hence the name 'Cinderdale')

5 *The path goes below the crag.*

C Viewpoint from narrow peninsula. Here the rock is harder and it resisted the sideways pressure of the grinding ice, which did have its effect downwards, as the lake is deep at this point.

6 *Follow path up and away from the lake, but close to the beck.*

7 *Cross beck and follow the right bank of the second beck which comes from Scale Force.*

8 *Cross the little bridge and the falls can be approached.*

D The falls spill down a fault. Note the evidence of mining activity from the remains of a waste heap.

9 *Follow the path down, past old sheep pen.*

10 *Path junction. Way becomes clearer.*

11 *Path meanders through wet sections.*

12 *Cross stone bridge and on to the hamlet.*

13 *Turn left and walk alongside the road.*

14 *Take the loop of an old road on the right.*

15 *Leave the road on the path above.*

16 *Take care on path corners.*

E Rannerdale Knotts. An excellent viewpoint.

17 *Take zig-zag down to the road.*

18 *Walk alongside the road to the starting point.*

ROUND BUTTERMERE

4 miles (6.4 km) Easy

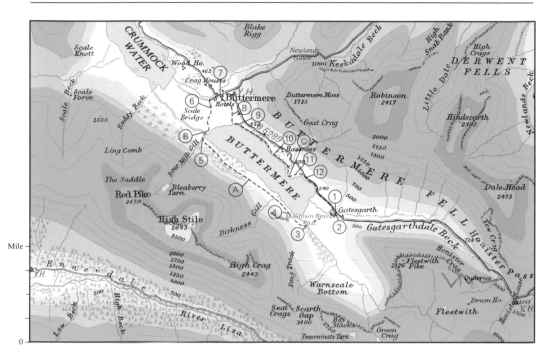

Many regard the walk round Buttermere as one of the best in the National Park. This lovely lake, originally belonging to Buthar the Norseman is set in a craggy tree-clad bowl. At its head is Fleetwith Pike towering above Honister Pass, and to the south the curved ridges of High Crag and High Stile, with their two great hollows and craggy arms which seem to be reaching out to embrace the lake. At the lake foot the steep wall of Red Pike scored with the slim silver line of Sour Milk Gill. The lake can be wild when windy, shimmery in the sunshine and sometimes calm and unaccountably dark green. The walk round is as easy on the feet as it is on

the eye, and as you are, on both shores, on public access land it is possible to picnic, and dawdle to savour the natural peace. Children will enjoy the surprise when the path goes through a rock tunnel.

1 *The walk starts at Gatesgarth. If there is no room in the little car park it is usually possible to find further parking spots on the Honister side.*
2 *Walk on the path past the farmyard and follow it by a fence across a field.*
3 *Cross the bridge and turn right.*
4 *Pick up the lakeshore path.*
A *National Trust land; you can wander here at will.*
5 *Turn right over bridge.*
B *Good view up the lake, and back*

to the long line of Sour Milk Gill.
6 *Follow the track on and through the hamlet of Buttermere.*
7 *Path goes right, just after joining road, and between farm buildings.*
8 *Path turns to go down a rocky bank to pick up the lakeshore path.*
9 *Follow the lakeshore at lake level or higher.*
10 *Path goes through a rock tunnel.*
C Shingle Point (National Park) A classic viewpoint. Opposite is High Crag left, and High Stile right. Good views framed by Scots Pines. Fleetwith Pike towers above the lake head.
11 *Path returns to the road.*
12 *Walk beside the road to the starting point.*

DERWENTWATER WEST SHORE

3 miles (4.8 km) Easy

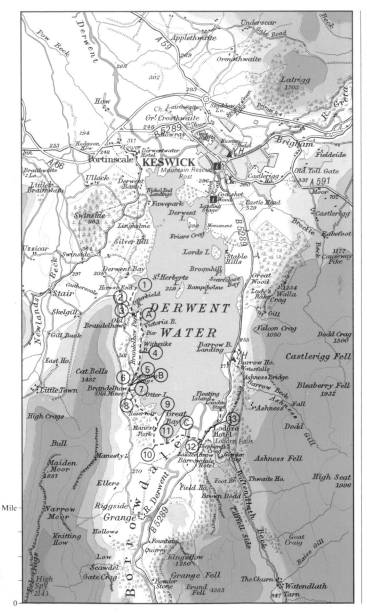

Keswick was once an important industrial town, black with smoke and at night glowing red from its furnaces. It seems hard to believe that in the mining boom years of the 18th century the whole area must have looked like an early Klondyke. The lake was a highway bringing charcoal from the ravaged woods as well as the ores from the western shores at Newlands and Cat Bells, Busy Brandley, or Brandlehow mine was at the lake's head. The mines have long since closed, trees have been allowed to grow again and the more kindly hand of man has healed what could only have been in a landscape of this scale, superficial wounds. Derwentwater, now a lush and beautiful setting, is largely in the care of The National Trust. From its jetties no longer is ore loaded, but people, who can enjoy the regular boat service that encircles the lake, giving walkers an opportunity to walk and picnic on the lakeside paths.

This walk uses the boat service to avoid road walking. Walkers need to take the boat to Hawse End landing, and be picked up at the Lodore. (Anti-clockwise service). Timetables are available from information centres.

1 *Disembark at Hawse End and follow the lakeshore footpath left.*
2 *Path leaves shore temporarily through stile and along field edge.*
3 *Turn left at end of the field to go over a plank walk and back to the shore. Follow the lakeshore path.*
A View over lake. St Herbert's

Over

Island is the nearest. This is said to be where the saint had his hermitage. Legend has it that he was such a close friend of St Cuthbert of Lindisfarne that they vowed they would die on the same day, which they did in AD687.

Opposite is Walla Crag. The west shore of the lake is in the softer geological area of the Skiddaw Slate, but opposite a notable contrast is the hard and craggy rock of the Borrowdale Volcanic.

4 *Keep to the lake edge path.*

5 *At the landing stage bear right.*

B Brandley mine used to be here but, now one can detect only the waste heaps of the operation which was started in ancient times when without gunpowder, the ore was worked by hand. Work continued like that for centuries, but in 1848 the Keswick Mining Company put in a 30ft (9.14m) water wheel. This proved inadequate for pumping so it was used for crushing and a steam engine was installed, which worked day and night for fifteen years! When the engine finally gave up the mine was temporarily abandoned before a new company was formed who put in a new 50hp engine, which in turn was replaced by a 350hp beam engine in 1888. The ore from the mine contained up to 83.5 per cent of lead and nine ounces (255g) of silver per ton.

6 *Fork. Bear left and up steps.*

7 *Through kissing gate and left between cottage and boathouse.*

8 *At fork, keep right. (Left is a private drive).*

9 *The land is boggy here, but it can be avoided by taking a long sweep to the right.*

10 *Join another path and go left to the shore again.*

11 *Follow the path going over walkways and bridges.*

C Good view over length of lake. Skiddaw is right at the lake head. As you turn to look at the path ahead the crag is Shepherd's and it is likely that climbers will be seen on it.

12 *Join road and turn left.*

13 *After Lodore Hotel take path on the left to the landing stage.*

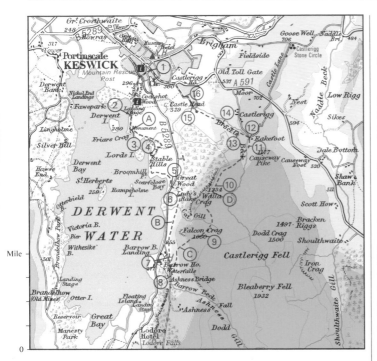

No other part of Britain can offer so many superb views in so small a area. Walla Crag is one of the more spectacular with views over the whole of Derwentwater to Bassenthwaite Lake, up into the jaws of Borrowdale, and to most of the major mountains. The walk is fairly strenuous but the reasonably fit can do it with no trouble; some people will take longer than others. There is plenty to see if the weather is clear; if visibility is poor the walk should not be attempted. It is advisable to carry some food with you. Strong footwear with good ground grip is necessary. The walk starts along Derwentwater shore.

1 The walk starts in Keswick. Walk down to the boat landings.

2 Continues on the pathway to its end.

A Friars Crag - a much photographed view up the lake and into the jaws of Borrowdale. Here, it is said, friars would wait to obtain a blessing from St Herbert. The saint lived in his hermitage on St Herbert's island in the 7th century.

3 Continue on the path round the bay and beyond The Ings.

4 Walk down to the lakeshore again by Stable Hills, and round Calf Close Bay.

5 Follow the path to the road, through a gap, and across the road into Great

Wood opposite. Continue up in the wood until the car park is reached. Join another path here.

6 There is a stile and sign to 'Ashness'. Follow this recently made path along the hillside.

B All praise to The National Trust for this path which reveals such splendid views over the lake.

7 The path joins a minor road to Ashness. Turn left up it.

8 Near an old gateway (before reaching stone-arched Ashness Bridge) a path starts on the left. Follow this up the fell.

C Good view over Derwentwater to Bassenthwaite.

9 Path junction. Continue straight on.

D The summit. Derwentwater is visible in all its splendour at a dizzy depth below. Behind is Causey Pike and to the right and beyond is Grisedale Pike. Look left up Borrowdale to see Scafell Pike, Scafell, and Great Gable. The Skiddaw range and Saddleback are towards the right and with your back to the cairn the Helvellyn range is in full view to the south-east.

10 Walk on from the cairn on a path downwards following a fence. Follow it on to a bridge.

11 Cross bridge and on to a metalled road. Follow it on.

12 Go left over the footbridge.

13 Continue right on pathway.

14 Path junction. Continue straight on.

15 Join roadway.

16 At this point a detour left is recomended to take in yet another viewpoint from Castlehead, a remarkable boss of rock overlooking the lake.

17 Return to roadway and back to starting point.

Walk 8
LODORE, WATENDLATH AND ASHNESS
4½ miles (7.2 km) 600 ft (182.8 m) Moderate; some wet areas

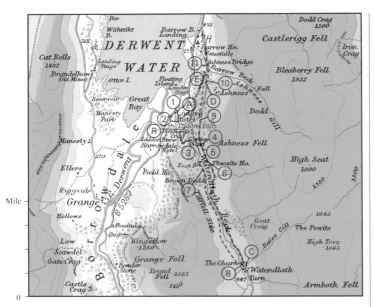

1 *Walk to the gate for the Lodore Falls just past the Lodore Hotel, and pay the nominal entrance fee. Go on to cross the bridge.*

A Choose your viewpoint. After heavy rain this is impressive. There are several drops, the largest one being about 90ft (27.4m).

2 *Go upwards with the falls following the zig-zag.*

B Several views of the falls as the path is climbed, and views back to Derwentwater.

3 *Keep right with the beck on the right.*

4 *Path eventually becomes more distinct and bends left.*

5 *At the road turn right and continue.*

6 *Turn right off the road to descend and cross the footbridge.*

7 *Follow the beckside footpath, avoiding, by detours, any wet ground.*

C Watendlath, a tiny hamlet with its own little tarn, is in the care of The National Trust.

8 *Return by the minor road unless this is very busy as it can be at times, then consider returning by the beckside path.*

9 *Escape from the road if possible by walking in the woods alongside. Watch for, on the left hand side where crags come close to the road, the well-named viewpoint.*

D 'Surprise View'; a tree-framed eagle's eye view over Derwentwater to the north-western fells.

10 *Continue on to the bridge.*

E Ashness Bridge. The best view is upstream and many photographers take to the water, often unintentionally from over excitement!

11 *Follow the road down to the main road. Cross over to the boat landing.*

In the early exciting days of tourism, when travellers in their horse-drawn coaches, were advised to keep their voices low, lest the reverberations of sound brought down the Borrowdale crags upon their heads, no visit to that awe-inspiring valley was complete without the sight of the thunderous falls of Lodore. Southey later wrote his famous poem 'The Cataract of Lodore' from his *Rhymes for the Nursery* about the falls' descent from top to bottom. Watendlath was made popular by Hugh Walpole's bestselling 1920s novel, *Judith Paris,* which is set in the hamlet. Guides would point to Judith's house by the tarn, even though she existed only in fiction. Ashness Bridge, with the view of the upper part of Derwentwater beyond is one of the

most photographed and painted scenes in Britain, its neighbouring viewpoint 'Surprise View' however is more dramatic, and one of its surprises is that people rarely fall off the precipice on which it is perched. All these can be revealed in one walk.

Parking is a problem in the Borrowdale valley and it is suggested that the walk should start at Lodore after a bus ride there, or after a trip by service boat to the Lodore landing. The walk finishes at Ashness gate where it is possible to get a boat or bus back. However at quiet times it should be possible to park in the car park by the lakeshore half way between the Lodore and Ashness Gate (Kettlewell car park). From here you can walk to and from the start and finish. The walk described is from Lodore landing.

21

NADDLE FELL

4½ miles (7.2 km) Strenuous

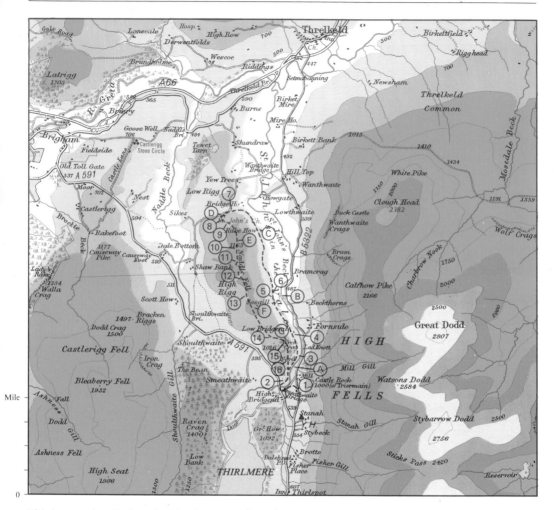

This is a superb walk for a fine day as it offers some spectacular alpine views. Naddle is a modest fell between the A591 road from Thirlmere to Keswick and the minor road up St John's in the Vale. There is the tiny isolated church of St John at one end and a glorious pine clad crag at the other; an airy rocky ridge with many superb prospects in between.

The walk is for people who are fit, even though it is only four and a half miles (7.2km) there is a steep ascent of 700ft (213.3m) and some rough terrain. Strong and well-cleated footwear is essential. It is best to treat this walk as whole day one, for there are many idyllic picnic and loitering spots. The walk starts fairly easily and pleasantly along the riverside. The difficult parts are in the middle and at the end.

Over

1 *Start at the Water Authority's car park and picnic area just a quarter of a mile (400m) north of Stanah, Thirlmere on the St John's (Penrith) road. Walk towards the picnic area by the river, but turn left down an abandoned road to the main Keswick road. Turn right along the verge and go over the bridge; then turn right over the stone stile onto the path. Continue for a short distance.*

2 *Take the left-hand path as signposted, then almost immediately go right at another junction to join a narrow but good path parallel with the river.*

A This is a delightful path on a wooded terrace with a good view of the river.

3 *The path nears the river by some giant boulders, then leaves it to follow the wall to the left.*

4 *At the gate climb left to go on the path above the buildings.*

5 *Divert right here for a viewpoint.*

B Sosgill Bridge, a fine stone arch with a view behind of Saddleback.

6 *Rejoin the path and continue to next viewpoint.*

C Rake How. Ruined farm.

7 *Join minor road and turn left.*

D St John's Church. The isolated situation may seem odd, but the road here was once well used. The first written reference to the church was dated 1554, but it is on the site of an earlier one. The existing building dates from 1845. The atmosphere inside is homely and friendly. Nearby is buried St John's best known personality, John Richardson (1817-1866) the talented dialect poet who helped to build the church.

8 *From the church and school there is a steep ascent to the left; but the recommended route for ease as well as to avoid encroaching on the privacy of the Youth Centre is to walk up on to the bank and along to the plantation fence, then left up to the kissing-gate on to the fell.*

9 *Go upwards on a grassy path to the ridge.*

E Summit cairn. Spectacular views over to Saddleback (Blencathra) (2847ft/867.7m), right; Skiddaw (3054ft/930.8m) left and to far left Grisedale Pike, Causey Pike and Bassenthwaite Lake.

10 *From the cairn follow the path on from the ridge. Deviate if you wish.*

This is open fell and there are detours to take in views.

11 *Path goes to the right of the wall and reaches a bog. This can be avoided by taking a wide sweep to the right, then left again under the face of a small crag.*

12 *Awkward stile over a wall. Follow the path bearing slightly left.*

13 *Make your way along the ridge.*

F Views. Helvellyn is ahead. Whiteside and Low Man almost obscure the summit at 3113ft (948.8m) beyond. Thirlmere is seen between the impressive wooded jaws of Great How and Raven Crag.

14 *To get off the ridge with as little difficulty as possible, first locate the gateway through the wall below, then walk on to the ridge end, before descending left to go through a gateway.*

15 *Walk on to the pine covered summit of Wren Crag.*

G Exciting views here framed in some beautifully sculpted Scots Pines.

16 *Descend steeply with path to rejoin path to starting path near the main road.*

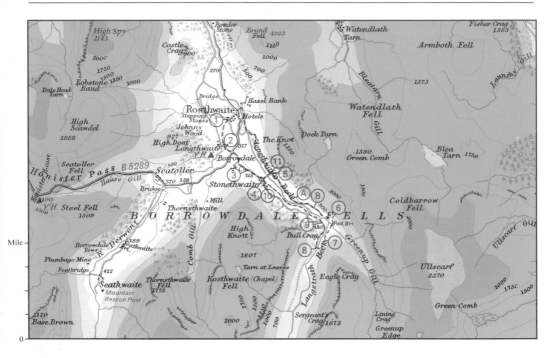

'The sight of this spot may calm a troubled spirit', so claimed the Sylvan in *Sylvan's Pictorial Handbook to the English Lakes* (1847). Stonethwaite is a tiny settlement which has given its name to a narrow valley containing the old pony-track routes to Grasmere via Greenup and Langdale via Stake Pass, which forks below the impressive hulk of Eagle Crag. Stonethwaite is well named ('thwaite' means a place, clearing or settlement), therefore literally this is a place of stones. There are millions of them brought down by the pounding fury of the often storm-swollen Langstrath Beck and Greenup Gill. At such times the place would hardly calm the 'troubl-ed spirit'. It is more often akin to an artillary bombardment.

The walk starts at Rosthwaite, if parking is available. If not, it is usually possible to park at point (3) on the walk.

1 *Walk down the lane running south-west from Rosthwaite and take the footpath going south, parallel with the river, from the fork.*

2 *At the bridge turn left down the lane; cross the road; go down the lane opposite and turn left at the old church and school.*

3 *Continue down the lane.*

4 *Turn left at the village; continue down the lane and cross the bridge.*

5 *Turn right after the bridge and follow the path by the riverside.*

A Good view of Eagle Crag. Bull Crag is across the valley.

B There is a force of water at this point.

6 *Pass the sheep pens then turn to cross the footbridge.*

7 *Wet ground can be avoided with care. Continue on and across the footbridge.*

8 *Turn right and follow pathway onto a stile.*

9 *Go into a field and follow the path by Stonethwaite Beck and across the fields to Stonethwaite.*

10 *Cross the bridge from the lane.*

11 *Turn left along the lane to Rosth-waite.*

24

Walk 11
HARROP TARN
2 miles (3.2 km) Moderate; wet areas

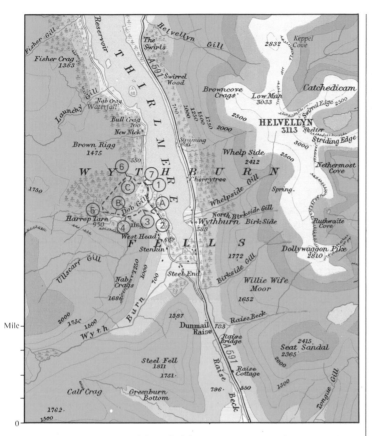

The walk starts at a small car park on the western minor road. Join this road at its junction with A591 (Ambleside to Keswick road), south of the lake. Follow this road for a mile (1.6km) to the end of a plantation on the left. The car park can be seen on a bank to the left.

1 *Leave the car park and walk south along the minor road.*

2 *Watch for the stile and signpost. Go upwards through the field to the left of the crag.*

A The crag is a fair viewpoint. The fell opposite is Helvellyn, but the summit is too far back to be seen. The track upwards in clear view is the popular route for walkers from Wythburn church.

3 *Walk upwards by a fence parallel with the beck which may be heard, if not seen, on the right.*

4 *Go through a stile and cross the beck, and walk on by the tarn.*

B Viewpoint over Harrop Tarn. Purists often condemn plantations of alien conifers; but here they certainly enhance the peaceful scene. One hopes that the peace will not be broken by the sight of a headless ghost said to haunt these parts!

5 *Turn right here on to the hard-surfaced forest track, and continue on ignoring joining tracks on right and left.*

6 *Turn left here by the stile for the forest and follow the zig-zag path down, parallel with the fence.*

C Best viewpoint here for Thirlmere and Helvellyn.

7 *Join road and turn right for the car park.*

There was once a long lake called Leathes Water in Thirlmere, which was spanned at its narrow waist by a stone bridge. By 1894 Manchester Corporation had acquired the valley and dammed the lake to raise it by 50 feet (15.2m), and the reservoir of Thirlmere was created, drowning the hamlets of Wythburn and Armboth. Only the higher-level chapel of Wythburn, to the east of the newly created road, now the A591, remains. An important packhorse route once ran from Wythburn (then known locally as 'the city') to Watendlath and Borrowdale. The first section is now only available to divers, but the rest still exists as a bridleway from the road on the west of the lake. The plantations, also put in by the Corporation, were once forbidden territory, but are now open to offer pleasant walks. This walk starts on the packhorse route to the tree-girt Harrop Tarn, returning through the forest.

AIRA FORCE

2 miles (3.2 km) Moderate; some slippery sections

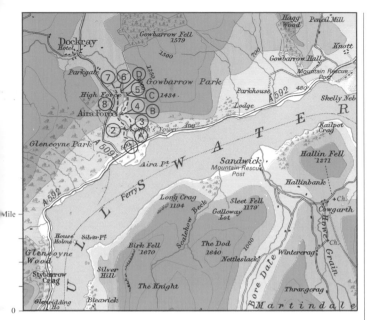

have done very well and do not detract from the scene. All this area is in the care of The National Trust.

3 *Turn left and go along a terraced path.*

4 *Go on to the bridge for a view up the falls. Then back on to the track to another bridge above. Come back again and go on up the path with great care.*

B View upwards from lower bridge reveals an 80 feet (24.4m) fall. The whole is enhanced by the tree and fern growth on the steep banks. The view from the second bridge reveals the fall dropping to the giddy depths below.

5 *Cross footbridge. Go up right alongside the bank with care.*

C The gill here flows down through a narrow channel.

D Another fall, High Force. This can be viewed from a point just above. Beware of slipping on the wet rock.

6 *Above the falls go through a stile in the wall on the left. Follow the feint path towards a stile and gate.*

7 *Just before this stile and gate go left on a footpath parallel to the wall.*

8 *There is a gate into the waterfall gorge enclosure. Go through this. A descent can be made to the falls again to return by the same route out, but the suggested alternative is to go right after the gate and up the wooden steps, not descending to the beck but continuing on by kissing-gate into the field to follow a path down to the starting point.*

There should be at least one walk suitable for a really wet day and this could be a good one, especially if the rain has given the high land a thorough soaking. The walker well protected by waterproofs, and partly sheltered by attractive woodland, can then enjoy the sight of an exciting fall of water, Aira Force by Ullswater. As Wordsworth described it 'A powerful brook, which dashes among rocks through a deep glen, hung on every side with a rich and happy intermixture of native wood -'. (1)

It is a short walk, but long enough in the rain. However, one might be inclined to take a lingering look at the unusual sight. Two important points *(a)* 'wellies' can be a liability on the slippery wet rock

and *(b)* dogs are not allowed on the permitted footpaths through the fields at the lambing season, and should be on leads in the fields at all other times.

1 *A car park serves the falls to the east of the junction of the road from Dockray with the Ullswater shore road (A592). At the far end of the car join the permitted path. (Not a right of way but passage is permitted). The path goes forward to the field.*

2 *Turn right on the path into the wood; cross bridges and go up the bank opposite.*

A Wordsworth was an enthusiast for 'the intermixture of native wood' and abhorred the introduction of alien species. Here, however there are some alien conifers which

Reference

(1) Wordsworth W. *Guide to the English Lakes*. London, 1835.

GREENSIDE
3½ miles (5.6 km) Easy

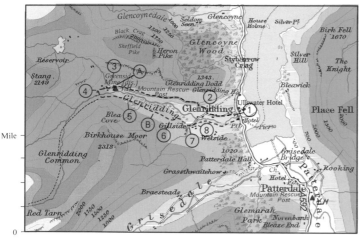

trees and further work is being done by the National Park Special Planning Board who now own the site. The walk uses the old mine track and a pleasant airy route following an old aqueduct.

Once Greenside, in an eastern valley of Helvellyn above the village of Glenridding, had one of the most profitable lead mines in the north of England. It was in production from the late 18th century to the middle of this one. It was reckoned that by 1876 it had produced some 40 000 tons (40 642 tonnes) of smelted lead, and 600 000 oz (24 000 g) of silver. In 1891 electrical winding gear was introduced. It was the first metal mine in the country to use it. The workings were extremely intensive and went deep into Helvellyn. An electrical locomotive (another first) was also used for drawing material from the productive shafts a mile (1.6 km) into the mountain. Originally this work was done by seven horses. Compressed air, for driving the drills, was provided by electricity. By modern standards the generating plant and installations were crude and dangerous, but they were worked with little mishap. Ore was smelted

on the site and the furnace flue was carried one and a half miles (2.4 km) up the mountain so that lead vapour could condense on the flue sides to be collected for return to the furnace. Water power was provided from the falls of Red Tarn and Kepple Cove Tarn above, the latter was dammed. This dam burst in a great storm in 1927 and a wall of water smashed through the workings and the village causing great damage, but miraculously no loss of life. The remaining sign of this disaster is the promontory on Ullswater formed from the debris and on which the steamer pier now stands.

Hardly anything remains of the works buildings and all is silent now. The mine was sealed in 1962 after the Atomic Energy Authority conducted seismic tests with conventional explosives deep in the workings. The old 'tailing dams' consisting of vast quantities of waste material were partly covered by the mining company, with grass and

1 *The walk starts at the Glenridding car park. Turn left and go up the road through the village estate.*

2 *Turn right at end of village, then left again on rough roadway past a line of terraced cottages and on up the valley via the track.*

A Little building on the right was the gunpowder store which was always situated well away from the main workings. Few other buildings remain; now two are being used as hostels. Note the stabilisation work on the surface of the tailing dams.

3 *Continue straight on up a track parallel to the beck which pounds dizzily below.*

4 *Cross footbridge to a path on other side of the beck and turn left on it.*

5 *Continue on the clear line of an old aqueduct which now makes a pleasant pathway.*

B Pleasant view left. The illusion is given that the walk on this aqueduct is down hill or level. In fact this is not so. Water was collected and taken back to the workings behind.

6 *Leave the aqueduct line and descend to the signed footpath below. Follow this path through.*

7 *The path joins the track, descend on it.*

8 *Do not cross the bridge, but turn on the riverside path back to village.*

CIRCUIT OF ENNERDALE WATER

7½ miles (12km) Fairly strenuous; some rough ground

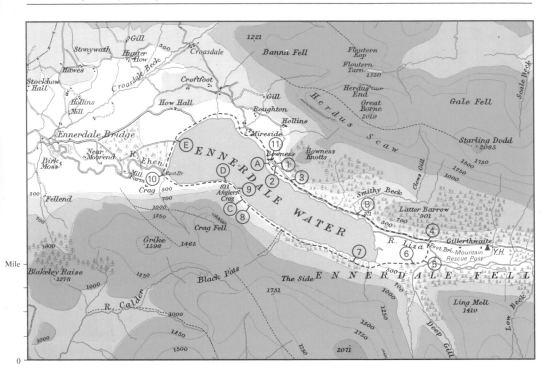

The views over Ennerdale Water suggest peace and awesome tranquility. Yet the dale has been the subject of heated controversy. There was very little when the lake was turned into a reservoir for this had minimal effect; but it was different when the Forestry Commission acquired most of the valley in the 1920s, displacing 2000 sheep and replacing them by many thousands of dark conifers, restricting free access to the area previously enjoyed by walkers. Despite protest the Forestry Commission won. More recently, in the 1980s, the Water Authority wished to raise the dam.

and flood a wide area. They were defeated by the combined weight of the Conservationists and the National Park Special Planning Board. If the Water Authority had won, this walk would have been impossible. Ennerdale is a deep crystal-clear lake. Around its head is the rock known as Ennerdale granophyre, a very hard mainly pink granite which breaks down into irregular blocks making walking, away from the made-up tracks, very uneven and thus more tiring than hazardous. The one apparent hazard on the walk is the steep side of Angling Crag. The path here is nar-

row but quite negotiable. This walk is adventurous and the memorable view across the lake, particularly upwards to the heights of Pillar and Steeple, are enough to set the senses tingling.

Strong, well-cleated footwear is essential. If the walk is to be savoured it is best to take a picnic lunch and spend most of the day on the walk. The walk begins at the car park provided by the Forestry Commission at Bowness Knott. To reach this, take the minor road from Croasdale north-east of Ennerdale Bridge.

Over

1 *Leave the car park and walk up the hill opposite, to the viewpoint.*

A Viewpoint here gives a superb view over the lake. Across the lake is Angling Crag. Contrast the view up the lake from here to the high fells, with the milder country down the lake. The high craggy land belongs to the Borrowdale Volcanic series of rocks. Around the upper part of the lake and behind us is the hard Ennerdale Granophyre, but down the lake are the soft shales of the Skiddaw Slates. When the moving ice of the Ice Age carved out the valley it was squeezed by the hard rocks, and then fanned out over the softer shale to give the lake its distinct shape.

2 *Walk down to the lakeshore. Continue left on the lakeshore path.*

3 *Join forest road and continue on.*

B 'Smithy Beck' suggests a rural industry now gone. In fact before the valley was depopulated, for the sake of timber and water supplies, the valley had been settled extensively since Viking incursions in the 10th century.

4 *Leave the road to cross the footbridge below.*

5 *Go right towards the lake head.*

6 *Go through the gate into the plantation and continue on the path.*

7 *Keep to the path on higher ground and avoid going to the lakeshore path too soon.*

8 *Go through the wall gap.*

C Viewpoint for lake head with Red Pike and High Stile to north.

9 *Path climbs to crag side over loose rocks, then falls below rock spur, and undulates before reaching an awkward step, then later down another. The path then descends to lakeshore.*

D The geological change should be seen on the shoreline here.

10 *Cross bridge and proceed along the causeway to pick up the lakeshore path.*

E Another splendid viewpoint which was once the site of the famous *Anglers Hotel* but now regretfully demolished under threat of eventual immersion.

11 *Follow the track leaving the lakeshore and return to the starting point.*

ULLSWATER SHORE WALK

6½ miles (10.5 km) Moderate

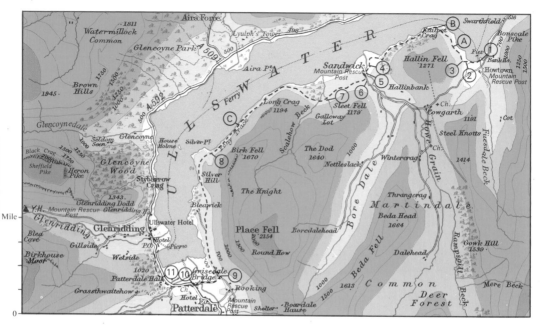

This is reckoned to be one of the Lake District's finest walks. It not only wanders close to Ullswater's shore but climbs gently to some sublime viewpoints. If a walk is worth doing it is worth doing slowly. Without doubt this is a dawdler's walk, with plenty of little havens for photographing, sketching, bird spotting or resting.

It is not a round walk. It starts properly at Howtown, on the east side of Ullswater and finishes at Glenridding on the south-west, so it is necessary to get a morning service yacht (Ullswater Navigation Company) from Glenridding pier to Howtown pier. Also take a packed lunch. There is a car park at Glenridding. Out of the season when the lake passenger service is not running, walkers need the aid of a helpful driver to take them round to Howtown and pick them up at Patterdale or Glenridding.

1 Leave Howtown pier and go immediately right to follow the path alongside the bay.

2 The path leaves the shore to climb the hillside to join a higher level path. Go right on it.

3 Follow the path round the headland.

A Good views north.

B Kailpot Crag. Ullswater contains shoals of a rare fish - the schelly (*Coregonus lavaretus*) - a sort of freshwater herring. Formerly the fish was netted in great quantities for food; a net was placed across here. The point opposite is appropriately named 'Skelly Neb'.

4 Path leaves the shore to cross the beck by a cottage.

5 Turn left for short distance on tarmacadam road.

6 Turn right after cottages to go on a path up bank following a wall side.

7 Keep right after bridges to the lake's side.

C Good views. Note the typical 'hanging valley' of Glencoynedale, that is one scooped out by glaciation in the side of Helvellyn.

8 Path junction, keep right. Path becomes track.

9 Turn right through farmyard to track beyond.

10 Turn right on road side.

11 When pavement ends, avoid walking on road by taking the footpath along the bank above on the left.

WASTWATER FOOT

5 miles (8km) Easy; some wet patches

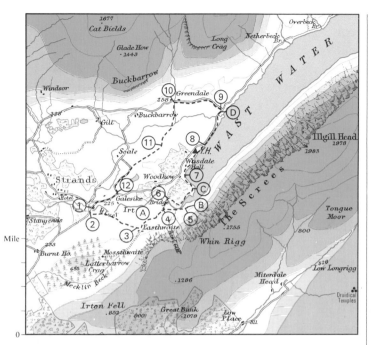

Many people visit Wastwater believing that it has an awesome and brooding, even slightly menacing, beauty. The massive line of steep screes crumbling some 1700ft (518.2m) down to the lake and then down a further 250ft (76.2m) below sea level into the darkness of the deepest lake in England. All that, with the heights of Great Gable and Scafell as stern and mute witnesses. Should you approach the view from Gosforth then all you have been told about its brooding, menacing beauty may well be confirmed. The screes instantly dominate your view on arrival. However, if you approach from the foot of the lake, with the screes end

on, the mass of water in front and that superb mountain backcloth beyond, then the view is very different. It is a classic at any time of year and can only be reached on foot. This walk takes in both views, with the latter from the lake foot first and the well-documented one second.

1 *East of the village of Strands (recently renamed Nether Wasdale) is a road junction. The walk starts at this point.*

2 *Two rights of way leave here from Santon Bridge road. Take the left-hand one signposted 'Easthwaite'.*

3 *Bear left at Easthwaite farm and go*

past farm buildings on to the path beyond.

A View up to the valley head.

4 *Path junction. Divert right to take in a view from the lake outflow.*

B View with the Screes towering above. The dominant fell in the background is Yewbarrow.

5 *Double back to path junction and go right, to the bridge.*

6 *After the bridge go right. Following the riverside path, and down to the lakeside.*

C Here is that view framed in trees. This is National Trust land and therefore you are permitted to stay and enjoy it at leisure.

7 *Continue close to the lakeshore and on in front of the Youth Hostel.*

8 *Join the road and walk alongside it.*

D This is the best known viewpoint. The screes were formed by action of glaciers in the Ice Age. The moving ice gouged out the lake bed and undermined the fell of Illgill Head behind. The unstable wall left has been crumbling and falling into the lake for many thousands of years since. There are still occasional substantial rockfalls and the cliff top is trenched with widening cracks. The deep ravines, out of reach of grazing sheep (and botanists!) contain some rare alpine plants and the area is scheduled as a Site of Special Scientific Interest.

9 *Turn away from the lake and down the Greendale road.*

10 *Bridge at Greendale. Turn left (signposted). Follow path through.*

11 *Path junction. Continue on. Path eventually goes on between the walls.*

12 *Join road and go right alongside it to starting point.*

ESKSIDE RAMBLE AND DALEGARTH WATERFALLS
4 miles (6.4km) Moderate; some rough sections.

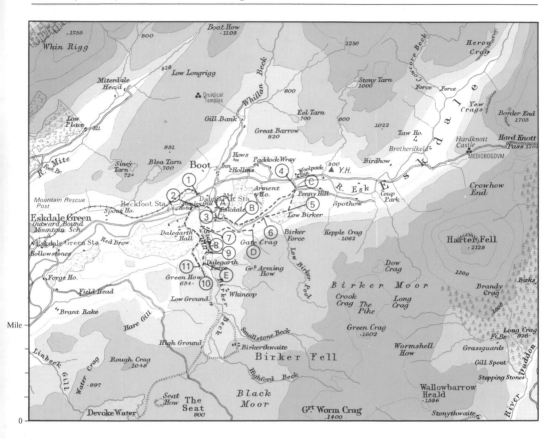

Eskdale lacks only a lake; but it has everything else. It is a long dale with its head under the highest land in England and its foot in the sea, and it has an incredible variety of landscape types. It would take a lifetime to explore it thoroughly. It has a history too. Down this dale came the stone axes roughed out by Neolithic craftsmen. They were then carried to the coastal sandstone for polishing and sharpening. The Romans improved the Anglo Saxon road and built a fort on one of the dale's spectacular vantage points, at Hardknott, and another to guard their port at the dale's foot at Ravenglass. Then followed the Viking settlements. After the Norman conquest the monks of Furness Abbey claimed much of the valley, managing the deer herds and probably opening the first iron mines here which produced high quality ore until the 19th century. The middle and lower reaches of the dale are walled by crags of granite, much of it coloured pink by the iron content. In one great wooded ravine in its southern side there flows a beautiful waterfall, known as both Dalegarth Falls and Stanley Ghyll Force. This walk follows the river side, past the dale's little church, and finishes by climbing up alongside the waterfall to an airy viewpoint on top of a precipice.

Over

32

1 *There are two possible starting points. One is at Dalegarth Station, the terminus of the narrow-gauge railway ('The Ratty') for anyone arriving by train from Ravenglass, or using the station car park. In which case it is necessary to walk a short distance back down the valley to the left turning by the little war memorial. The walk then begins at a turning left between the walls a little way along this road. Alternatively, the walk can be started from the car park down the Dalegarth road, walking back to cross the bridge. The path starts at the first turning on the right.*

2 *The path leads to St Catherine's Church.*

A A Chapel was established in Eskdale as long ago as the 12th century. In the 15th century the chapel was promoted to a parish church. This upgrading followed a successful petition to the Pope which complained about the hardships experienced in travelling to St Bees for burials and baptisms. The church was rebuilt in 1881. In the churchyard there are two interesting gravestones to two notable huntsmen, Tommy Dobson and Willy Porter.

3 *On leaving the church, follow the path left by the river bank.*

B There are some beautiful clear pools in the river bed. Look for the remains of a mine bridge for transport of the ore via the railway.

4 *Cross the stone bridge.*

C Attractive arch bridge of local stone.

5 *Just above Low Birker farm, turn right on to a clear track.*

6 *The track continues parallel with the river.*

D Signs of mining activity around include very red earth, and waste tips.

7 *Cross the bridge, walk up the bank and go left to follow the gill side to join clear path.*

8 *Cross two bridges.*

9 *Viewpoint bridge. The true path turns here, but the fit and agile might scramble a little further for more views of falls, but they must return to this point. Double back and go upwards from here turning left at a T-junction, over a little beck and up to a viewpoint.*

E Those with no head for heights will have to be content with standing back. *Children should be closely controlled.* The crag falls sheer into the gill at this point, but there is a grand view northwards over the Eskdale valley, which is framed by trees.

10 *Leave this viewpoint and follow the path to a stile over the wall, which joins a good track.*

11 *Turn right and follow the track past Dalegarth Hall to your starting point.*

MUNCASTER FELL

6¼ miles (10km) Strenuous; wet sections

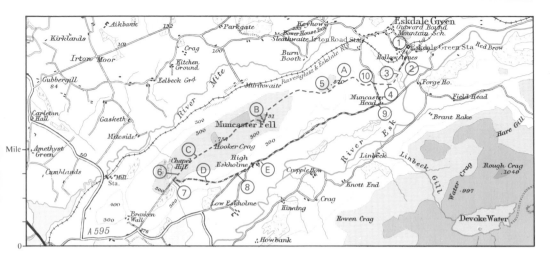

Between the lower reaches of Miterdale and Eskdale, separating the rivers Mite and Esk before they flow into the sea at Ravenglass, there is a long tongue of fell of modest height offering sea and fell views and an invigorating walk. Over this fell in 1461, so it is said, staggered the exhausted Henry VI, fleeing from his defeat by the Yorkists at far off Towton. He was found by shepherds and carried to Muncaster Castle, where he was hidden and cared for until it was safe to leave. To show his gratitude the King later gave a glass bowl 'The Luck of Muncaster' to his benefactor Sir John Pennington of Muncaster, and his successors later built a monument at the spot where the king was found. That is one legend; but there is another which indicates that the fell is haunted by an apparition of a distraught lady carrying the head of her lover. Her father's 'hit man' reputedly hacked it off to prevent her marrying beneath her station! The station of immediate concern though is a railway station, Eskdale Green, on the narrow gauge 'Ratty' railway, as it is the starting point for this walk.

1 *Park in Eskdale Green. If the village car parks are full go south, cross the bridge over the Esk, and park on a wide lay-by just beyond. The walk starts by the railway station and runs parallel to the line on the eastern side.*

2 *Junction. Keep left.*

3 *Go through the gate and over the beck. Follow the wall on the right.*

4 *Make for the gate on the side of the track ahead. Go through it and turn right for a short distance and then left for a fell track. Climb it.*

A Good view over the village of Eskdale Green. Beyond are the slopes of the Scafell range.

5 *Path skirts fellside, marked by stones.*

B Ross's camp. Not an ancient monument, but apparently erected for fun in 1883 where shooting parties stopped for picnics.

C View out to sea. If its clear the Isle of Man can be seen. Windscale, the Atomic Energy Authority's works are also apparent.

6 *Metalled road joined for a short distance. The tarn is visible on the right.*

7 *Turn left on the green path which soon skirts a wood.*

D The strange tower below is said to mark the spot where the shepherds found Henry VI.

8 *Go down to join hard-surfaced track. Turn left on it.*

E Almost certainly this is the line of the Roman road from Hardknott to Ravenglass. A Roman tile kiln was discovered here.

9 *Go left by the farmyard and through gate beyond.*

10 *Take care not to miss the gate on the right, through which you rejoin the path to starting point.*

DEVOKE WATER

3 miles (4.8km) Moderate; wet

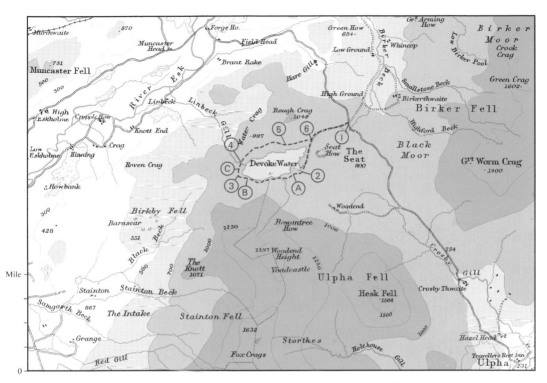

Archaeological evidence, and examination of pollen types found deep in the mud and peat, has shown that in prehistoric times the landscape around Devoke Water was forest, and that there was very extensive human settlement by Neolithic farmers or hunters. There are also many burial mounds and hut circles in the district. Since then climatic changes, and the hand of man has reduced the area to wild open moorland, and although Devoke Water is similar to Brotherswater in size it is now a placid tree-girt lake typical of the Lake District. It is a mountain tarn open to the sky, lashed by Atlantic winds its mood responds quickly to the changing weather. It has an untamed appeal and this walk around the tarn is a breezy one on rather sketchy paths but with the opportunity, for the adventurous, to pioneer their own routes. There are, however, boggy areas, the worst of which can be avoided with care. A good point to remember is that heather will not flourish on very wet ground.

1 *Park your car by the roadside by the minor road opposite the track for Devoke Water. Take the track signposted 'Waberthwaite'.*

2 *The path passes a track to the old boathouse.*

A Viewpoint.

B Viewpoint with Scafell range, Bowfell, and Langdale fells in background.

3 *Head round the lake heading for nearby higher ground.*

C Viewpoint west towards the sea and east over the lake, the fells above Eskdale and Dunnerdale.

4 *Cross the outlet with care. The way beyond is fairly pathless. Head for higher ground on the side of Water Crag.*

5 *The wet areas here are not too soft.*

6 *Rejoin track and return.*

35

HARDKNOTT ROMAN FORT AND HARDKNOTT FOREST
7 miles (11.3km) 1200ft (365.7m) Strenuous; steep; rough and boggy sections

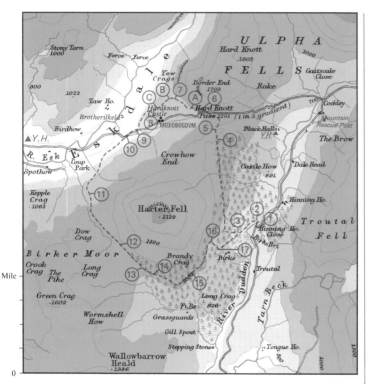

Eighteen centuries ago a cohort of Roman auxiliaries, many of them having made a long and hazardous slog all the way from what is now Yugoslavia, marched up the steep hump of Hardknott to undertake a formidable but necessary task; the building of a stone fort. They built it on an incredible site, perched on the mountainside high above Eskdale, defended by a precipice on its north and west and by a deep valley to the south. They could have given it a fittingly dramatic name like 'Eagle's Eyrie' or 'Heartbreak Hill'. Typically, however, they call-

ed it *Mediobogdum* meaning 'the middle of the bend'. There its ruin remains and none with even the smallest amount of imagination can fail to be stirred by it.

Many motorists, who risk damaging transmission systems and brakes on the steep and narrow hairpins of Hardknott Pass, pass by the fort without knowing of its existence. It is far better to walk there from the head of Dunnerdale and although the walk is a bit strenuous on the climb through Hardknott Forest, it will demonstrate just how tough and fit the Romans must

have been. The walk goes through some rather remote areas so it is necessary for lone walkers to leave word with someone about their route details. A person with a broken leg or ankle could lie around undiscovered for days.

1 *Park in the Forestry Commission's car park, south of Hinning House at the head of Dunnerdale.*

2 *At fork, keep left.*

3 *Path crossroads. Take path climbing up to the right. This is marked with green markers. Follow the path through the forest.*

4 *Leave the forest by the gate. (Close it afterwards) Bear right to follow the fence for a short distance, then onwards on the same line from the corner.*

5 *The path meanders on higher ground to the right of the tarn to avoid boggy areas, and then it emerges on the road. Turn left along it, taking care not to impede struggling motorists.*

6 *At the corner of extreme hairpin in the road, go right, on to the grassy path and on past two knolls.*

A Some good viewpoints of the fort. Parade ground is just in front and above the fort. It is a large area free of boulders. An enormous amount of slave labour must have been needed here!

7 *Path turns. At this point go down to cross the parade ground and then head for the northern (right-hand) wall of the castle ruin, to avoid the bog.*

B The Parade Ground. The ramp, where the commander would oversee his troops, is to the north (right).

Over

36

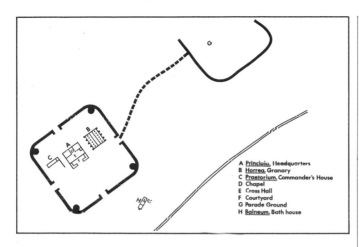

A **Principiu.** Headquarters
B **Horrea.** Granary
C **Praetorium.** Commander's House
D Chapel
E Cross Hall
F Courtyard
G Parade Ground
H **Balneum.** Bath house

C The fort lay-out follows classical lines. Every Roman commander must have been issued with the appropriate plan and manual! There had to be four gates, one in the centre of each wall, even though, in this case, the north gate opens, not onto a road but a precipice. The main gate is in the south wall, and above it was a stone slab, fragments of which were found in 1964. The inscription on it proclaimed that the fort was set up for Emperor Caesar Trajan Hadrian Augustus, by the fourth cohort of Dalmations. The slab was of slate which must have been carried over from Langdale. Sandstone facings here too must have been carried from the coast. The walls were some 12ft (3.6m) high topped with a sentry walkway and battlements. At each corner were higher stone towers. Much of the stone has been carted away over the centuries to provide cheap building material.

The fort would have had most of the interior space filled with buildings, mainly of wood, to house some 500 men. The foundations of the stone buildings remain. In the centre, is the *Principia*, (the headquarters building) with the usual open courtyard in front and walled by two L-shaped chambers. Behind this is the cross hall which would have been roofed. This is where the officers assembled to receive their daily orders, and behind this are three chambers, the centre one being the chapel, with offices on either side. To the right of the *Principia* was the other very necessary stone building used for storing grain. On the other side was the commander's house.

Do not miss the airy view over Eskdale to the Scafells, from the precipice outside the north gate. Eskdale, like Hardknott Pass, was probably an important British trade route to the ancient port of Ravenglass at the dale foot. The routes were 'improved' by the Romans,

who took over the port, and built the important fort, 'Glannaventa'.

Even in a remote spot such as this the Romans had to have their bath. Here, it is outside and below the main gate.

8 *Leave the fort by the west gate. Walk on following the grassy path (some of it is part of the Roman road) to the wall, then turn left with the wall to join the roadside.*

9 *Descend on to the roadside.*

10 *Just before the cattle grid cross the beck by a little stone bridge and climb up the good built-up track to the left.*

11 *After passing through the gate onto open fell, stop. The built-up path soon ends. Ignore the good path going on and up the fell to the left.* **Go right** *on an obscure path following the fence which is on the right. This path is very feint in places but an occasional look right at the fence will keep you on the right line as it runs roughly parallel.*

12 *Enter the forest through the gate (close it afterwards). The way on is waymarked in blue.*

13 *When path comes close to the forest road end and vehicle turning bay take care! Path forks just below it. Go left here on 'blue route'.*

14 *The path joins the forest road for a short distance.*

15 *When forest road bends sharp right* **keep straight on.** *A blue marker should be seen ahead. This path is not too clear at first but gets better and is a pleasant walk.*

16 *Path junction. Go right.*

17 *Join the forest road. Leave the blue route here and go left to the starting point.*

BIRKS BRIDGE AND SEATHWAITE, DUNNERDALE

6 miles (9.6km) Moderate

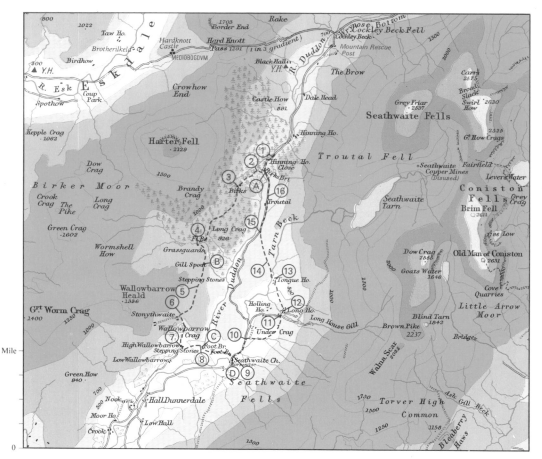

Of all the Lake District rivers the Duddon is surely the most sublime. Wordsworth thought so and wrote a poem entitled *The River Duddon*, from which this stanza is taken.

'All hail, ye mountains: hail,
      thou morning light!
Better to breathe at large on this
      clear height
Than toil in the needless
      sleep from dream to dream:

Pure flow the verse, pure,
      vigorous, free and bright,
For Duddon, long-loved
      Duddon, is my theme!'

   The Duddon rises on the fells above Wrynose and can be a gentle flow or a frenzied torrent. The valley it flows through is tree clad, green and serene. This walk starts above the famous Birks Bridge.

1 *Park in the Forestry Commission*
car park near the valley head, and walk back down the road.

A The bridge here is a thing of beauty itself, but do look into the green water and see how the torrent and spinning stones have sculpted the hard bed rock.

2 *Cross the bridge and take the path going right then turn sharp left to the Birks.*

Over

3 *Keep left on the forest tracks and cross the footbridge to Grassguards.*

4 *Go through the yard and down the track between the walls.*

B Look at the drystone walls on either side of the track; a beautiful example of the waller's art.

5 *Path to an open fell.*

6 *Just before Stoneythwaite farm go left to follow the wall and which falls steeply to High Wallowbarrow.*

7 *Go towards the farm, then turn left alongside the barn and go through the stile to pick up the path on the grassy terrace left.*

C Some pretty rock pools here under the fine arched bridge.

8 *Go over the bridge, walk up the path by the wall and over a slate bridge, then on to cross an old mill race by another. Continue on the path and cross two more bridges to the roadside and Seathwaite Church.*

D No visit to Seathwaite is complete without learning about 'Wonderful Walker' who lived here as curate of the little church for 66 years and died in 1802 at the age of 92. His stipend was £50 *per annum*, and yet, despite giving to the poor, he still had £200 left in his will. He worked hard as an itinerant farm worker, taught the children and healed the sick. There is a brass plate to his memory on the wall. The stone where he sat to shear sheep is in the yard not far from his wife's grave. She lived until she was 81

9 *Go up the road.*

10 *Take the turning right for Turner Hall. On this road continue on but ignore the right turn. On reaching the T-junction turn left and go directly on a track ignoring the right turn. Keep left of the buildings.*

11 *Join the road and go left and immediately turn sharp right and towards Long House.*

12 *Cross the bridge and turn sharp left on the path between the walls. Go through the stile and over the bridge to Tongue House farmyard.*

13 *Go forward to the road, turn left for a short distance, then cross the footbridge on the right. Follow the wall by the catwalk. Walk in front of the house by the wood and then cross over the stile. Climb up through the woods.*

14 *Follow the incline right over the hillside on green path. The path is less distinct, but walk on towards Harter Fell ahead. Cross over the stile and descend to the road.*

15 *Go right on the road.*

16 *Pick up riverside path to Birks Bridge, then follow the road to the car park.*

LOWER DUDDON AND FRITH HALL

5 miles (8km) Moderate

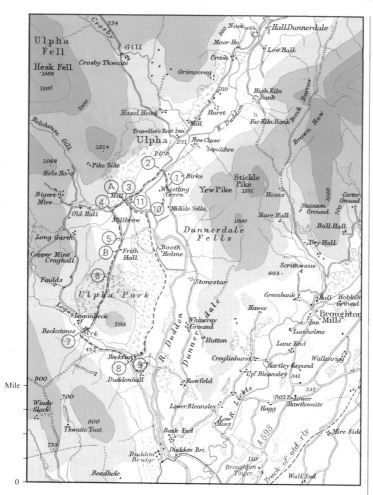

1730 seventeen marriages were recorded. In 1736 a guest met a mysterious end. He was possibly murdered. His ghost is said to haunt the place.

1 *The walk starts south of Ulpha Bridge. A parking space can usually be found by the roadside. Walk to the bridge.*

2 *Cross the bridge and turn left along the road.*

3 *Just after the second bridge on this road note what was once a mill on the right. Continue on.*

A Much use was made of the running water in these valleys. Here at one time timber from the surrounding coppice woods, was turned to provide bobbins for the Lancashire textile industry.

4 *After the road levels out look for a small bridle gate to the left. Go through this and follow the wall.*

5 *Cross the stile in the wall. Join the track and turn right, go over bridge and on.*

B Frith Hall ruin. Good views from a very 'atmospheric' prospect.

6 *Continue down the old track which becomes pleasant walking. The track descends to the road.*

7 *Turn left and follow the road down.*

8 *Go left down the track (signed as Mill Bridge and Mill How) towards the houses, over a bridge.*

9 *Go over a second bridge, by the farmyard and down a track through trees, which follows on by the woodland and plantations. Wet areas can be avoided with care.*

10 *The track curves left.*

11 *Join the road and go right to the starting point.*

The River Duddon is a delight throughout its route. Two roads, either side of the Duddon's lower reaches join at Ulpha (Scandinavian 'ulf-hauga' meaning 'wolf hill'). On whichever road you travel your eyes are drawn to a ruined 'castle' on the hill between. This is Frith Hall, high on the ancient roadway. It is not a castle, but a former hunting lodge for the Ulpha deer park owned by the Huddleston family. At the end of the 16th century it became an Inn. In the 18th century the Inn got itself a reputation. It became a sort of 'Gretna Green'; in

LANGDALES AND BLEA TARN

8 miles (12.9km) Strenuous; some wet places

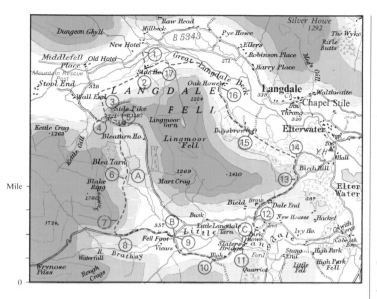

A Detour left to the foot of tarn for view over to Langdale Pikes.

6 *Continue on the footpath from the tarn. It is undulating and rough in places.*

7 *Continue on path here, avoid temptation to take short cut - swamp!*

8 *Join the roadside and go left downwards with it to pass a farm.*

B Stone bridge. Another viewpoint for Pikes.

9 *Cross stone bridge and go along the track.*

10 *Junction. Keep left to go past the buildings and quarry spoil heaps.*

11 *Look for the bridge on the left, go through the stile and follow the path over the bridge.*

C An interesting bridge which is thought to be quite ancient; a splendid example of the bridge builder's art.

12 *Join the road, go left for short distance, then right, on a track between the walls.*

13 *Take care here. Go through the gate and then go up immediately left into wood. Keep on the path right of the wall avoiding the quarry lane left.*

14 *The path joins the quarry road. Go left.*

15 *Baysbrown Farm. Go on past it on the quarry road for a short distance, then walk down through the wood to follow a path past Baysbrown towards Oak Howe.*

16 *Avoid wetness as best you can on higher ground, go left of Oak Howe to follow the riverside for short distance, then over a ladder stile to join the path to Side House Farm.*

17 *Rejoin the track from Side House for the starting point.*

The Langdale Pikes, from whichever of the hundred viewpoints they are seen are the most distinctive fell feature of the Lakeland landscape, and Great Langdale is the largest attraction on offer for serious fell walkers and climbers. But there is a superb lower-level walk taking in both Great and Little Langdale; a delight all the way. This walk starts under the Pikes themselves and goes via probably their best viewpoint, Blea Tarn; This view is captured in a poem by Wordsworth 'Little lowly vale, a lowly vale, and yet uplifted high among the mountains' (*The Excursion*) But there are other viewpoints from Little Langdale and Great Langdale's lower reaches. Photographers could go mad with delight on this walk; but might be in danger of collapse if they carry heavy equipment as there is steep

ground to cover early in the walk.

1 *Start from one of the public car parks just up-valley from the Dungeon Ghyll New Hotel. (There is a larger car park behind the trees on the right). Join the road, walk up the valley for a short distance then take the track left to walk just beyond Side House Farm.*

2 *Turn right on the contouring footpath and follow it through to the plantation.*

3 *Go left, upwards with the fence, round the edge of the plantation, through the gate or over stile. Follow the contour above the plantation and at the end of it go through the gate and up the left. (Steep)*

4 *Path comes close to the road. Go on with it alongside road to a stile.*

5 *Cross the stile onto the road, and cross it to join a path opposite to Blea Tarn.*

TILBERTHWAITE AND LITTLE LANGDALE

4 miles (6.4km) 1000ft (304.8km) Moderate; some very steep, rough, wet sections

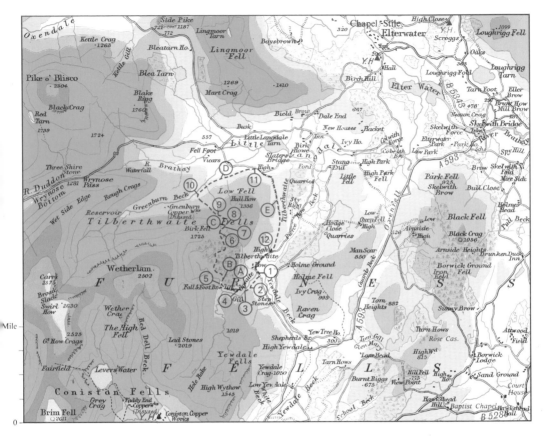

There is some steep ground on this route so sandals, wellington boots or smooth-soled shoes are out. Remember that steep grass can be as treacherous as rock. Old mine shafts are another hazard for those whose curiosity may lure them from the path; though the more dangerous ones are fenced. Children and dogs should be kept carefully controlled. Lone walkers should take the precaution of leaving route details with someone at 'base'. Although this walk has these disadvantages the rewards are great. It starts by the waterfall, which is very spectacular after rain and goes via ancient copper mines. After making the ascent to the walk's highest point any breath left could be taken away by the awesome, symphonic (Wagnerian?) view over Langdale.

1 *Park in the old quarry parking area at the foot of Tilberthwaite Gill, which is reached by a minor road off the Coniston to Ambleside road. As-* *cend by the path rising on the left-hand side of the gill, following the gill's course at the higher level.*

2 *Bear right and descend to cross the gill by the footbridge. Then follow rough scrambly path and stone steps to the bridge.*

A Viewpoint. The fall seen here is only 20 feet (6m) but the volume of water is often very great. The upper falls cannot be reached. Earlier this century more bridges and catwalks

Over

were in position above this view-point bridge, but they have been swept away by massive floods which have torn down the unstable walls of the ravine.

3 *Go back from the viewpoint bridge some 16 yards (14.6 m) then climb up the narrow rough path which rises steeply to the left.*

4 *Follow this path upwards, over a stile, to join the old miners' track. Go left up it.*

5 *At top of the gill ravine, go right on the old miners' track.*

B Everywhere there are signs of copper mine workings; spoil heaps and ruins. The veins of ore going east and west here have been exploited since ancient times. This side of the Coniston Old Man range is riddled with holes like a maggoty cheese. There is some evidence that copper was mined here in Roman times, though inevitably many of the signs of old workings have been destroyed by more recent activity. The last major efforts in this area, including the driving of a 500 fathom level (914m), and the sinking of a 65 fathom shaft (118.87m), occurred in 1850, but extraction proved too costly and the main production became concentrated in the Coniston Copper Mines to the south-west, and at Greenburn to the north.

6 *At this point, near the old mine workings and stonework where the track goes sharply left for a steep (and eroded) ascent to Wetherlam,* **go right,** *upwards on a less distinct path past old mine workings and stonework. Beware of the collapsed and dangerous shaft.*

7 *At the top of this 'saddle' look directly below to see a fairly indistinct path to the right of a fence and a bog. Take care on this steep descent.*

C There are many fine views of Langdale Pikes but surely none to cap this! Sit here and look. In the foreground there is a tumble of crags and between Blake Rigg and Lingmoor, Blea Tarn can be seen. This is the type of landscape which burst like a bomb on the early tourists' eyes in their discovery of the Lake District in the 18th century. 'Langdale Pikes hold their ragged heads in shapeless horror' wrote Budworth in a book at that time. 'Horror' was a popular word for the writers of the day when describing the district. Then, it was used to mean excitement rather than terror. Perhaps television and easy travel today has made us rather more blasé about scenery. But this view cannot fail to stir. It is surely one of the best mountain prospects in Britain.

8 *Go over the stile and walk on the right. Follow wall down to a high step stile.*

9 *Go over this, then go left of beck and follow wall, with care, by the steep fragmentary path interspersed with grass tussocks and wet ground.*

10 *Join the miners' track and go right.*

D Enjoy further marvellous views over to Langdale Pikes. Here the foreground is a rocky chaos, a turmoil of craggy shapes, adding more drama. Forward is Little Langdale Tarn. The road over Wrynose begins below in Little Langdale. The modern road follows the old Roman road (the Xth iter) over the pass, linking the fort at Ambleside with the fort at Hardknott and on to Ravenglass. Its route until it reaches the farm of Fell Foot below is not traceable, but from there onwards it is to the north, that is the far side, of the present road.

11 *Track junction. Go upwards to the right and follow the quarry track straight onwards (detours lead to quarries).*

E Extensive quarrying to the right. The quarrying boom followed the copper mining. To win the copper the mining engineers had to break through the very hard volcanic rock. When the copper prices fell because of cheap imports, and the steel shipbuilding lessened the demand for copper plates which sheathed the hulls of wooden vessels, the sales potential of the fine hard slate was realised. The mine waste heaps became buried under quarry waste as the boom continued. Sometimes the slate was actually mined, when the levels of higher class material were followed into the mountain side. A detour to look at the slate might be of interest. The colour varies in each locality. The material was formed from volcanic dust laid down under water and the ripple marks can sometimes be seen. The slate is hard and takes a good polish. In the boom in the 19th century records show that a quarryman was paid a guinea (£1.05) for working a six day week.

12 *The track finishes at a gate (close it afterwards) and a surfaced lane is reached. Go right, by the farm, to the starting point.*

TORVER BACK COMMON AND CONISTON WATER SHORE

3½ miles (5.6km) Moderate; some wet sections

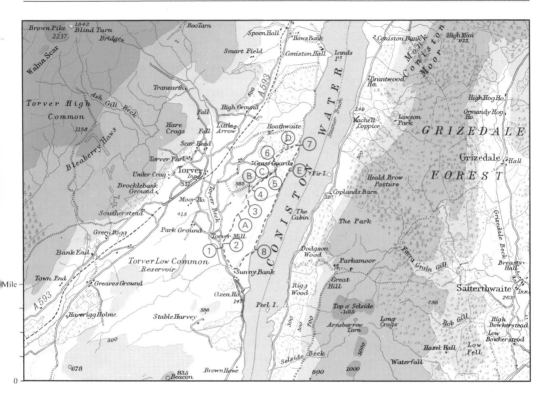

It is not generally known that there is pedestrian access either by right of way or on public access land, to most of the western shore of Coniston Water. This reveals views unknown to the general tourist, away from traffic noise and bustle. Fast boats too are not present on Coniston Water as there is a ten miles (16km) per hour speed limit. This makes it more attractive than Windermere for those who look for serenity. This is an away-from-it-all walk on common land with excellent views, finishing on a lake shore path.

1 *The walk starts from the Coniston to Ulverston road one mile (1.6km) south of Torver. There is a large lay-by parking area here opposite a large garage. Walk on from this point, through a gate, and left of the little tarn. Walk on the grassy path with the wall on the left.*

2 *At the wall corner a rushy tarn should be seen ahead. Take the path up the hill to the right of it.*

A Viewpoint above the tarn. Excellent view of Coniston Old Man range and a stretch of the lake. All this is common land. Many years ago this would have been wooded,

but the trees have been cleared and the land grazed by sheep. Now most of the land is covered with bracken which spreads rapidly in deep-soiled open land and is almost impossible to eradicate. The grazing area is now very limited. Only a few trees survive here as seedlings are soon eaten by sheep. Here there are a few mountain ash (rowan).

3 *Looking up the lake from the viewpoint a path will be seen descending to the end of the tarn. It goes over a hump of land beyond, and on to a small crag. Follow this path.*

Over

B This viewpoint gives a perfect view of the Old Man range and there is a small natural stone seat facing it. The view over the lake goes right to the head, and away to the north is the Helvellyn range.

4 *Walk on the path through the bracken from the viewpoint. The path meanders slightly, then goes between juniper bushes to descend a bank.*

C Junipers are getting scarcer in many parts of the country but they still survive in the Lake District. Juniper is our only native cypress. Note the varied shapes of the shrubs here; some are quite old. Chew the berries, whether green or ripe, and you will find out how gin gets its flavour. The berries have long been valued in medicine.

5 *After descending the bank, go down the gully to the right for a short distance, and then pick up the distinct path which leaves it on the left. Follow this path on to a junction.*

6 *Turn right down the path.*

D The path goes through woodland which was once coppiced, that is cut every 12 years or so, and new growth allowed to come from the 'stools' (stumps). Formerly these woods were used to supply charcoal for the iron furnaces; mainly oak, alder and birch.

7 *The path eventually reaches the lakeshore, turn right to follow clear path by the lake.*

E Two things to look for on the shoreline. There is clinker which will show where 'bloomeries', small 'do-it-yourself' smelting operations were carried out here in ancient times. Ore was brought by boat to points where charcoal was readily available. In boggy areas there are insect-eating plants; the butterwort, and the sundew. They are small plants, easily missed, but once identified can be observed in many places. There are a number of good viewpoints along the shore.

8 *Path eventually leaves the shore to climb a bank before reaching the wall boundary to the common. This path leads to the road. Turn right and walk alongside it to the starting point.*

HOLME FELL
4 miles (6.4km) 740ft (225.5m) Strenuous; rough sections

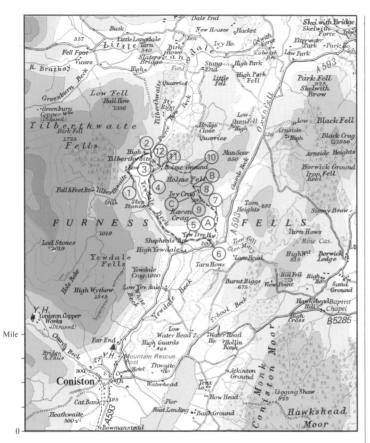

Ambleside it is the second turning on the right after passing the little road side tarn; Yew Tree Tarn.

2 Walk on to High Tilberthwaite Farm, going right, through the gate immediately in front of the buildings.

3 The path forks. Continue on.

4 Join minor road, turn right along it and walk on all the way with the river on the right.

5 Turn left just before the bridge. Go up the path by the wall.

6 When the wall finishes go left before the gate and follow the path upwards. It starts with a wall on the right, then the path veers left.

A View over Yew Tree Tarn

7 At the big boulder bear left to go upwards on loose surface.

B View over Langdale Pikes

8 Just as the path starts to descend, go left to the big stone cairn visible above. This marks Ivy Crag Summit.

C Rest by the cairn and enjoy the view which, by any standards, is spectacular.

9 Do not be tempted into exploration. There are some dangerous crags to the south. Turn back to the path junction, at (8) and turn left, towards the little tarn.

10 Go left just before the tarn. Then afterwards bear left towards another little tarn. Go left again under the trees to join path at the T-junction, then right on path which becomes more distinct.

11 At wall turn left, through the gate and descend. Turn sharp right down to the cottages.

12 Walk past the cottages then turn right down a footpath to High Tilberthwaite and back to the start.

Holme Fell is a craggy fell wedged between the northern spur of the Coniston Old Man range, and the hills around Tarn Hows. Although modest in height, it is an exciting summit, rough, humpy and scrubby, with a thrilling view over to Langdale, to Helvellyn and Fairfield and High Street, but particularly near at hand is the great bulk of Wetherlam. There is a pleasant feeling of wildness and isolation and possibly an exaggerated sense of achievement in the adventurous final scramble up to Ivy Crag.

Obviously strong footwear is required for this walk, which should not be attempted in bad weather.

1 Park at the foot of Tibberthwaite Gill. To get there turn left at the first turning going north from Coniston towards Ambleside. Or from

TORVER LOW COMMON

2½ miles (4km) Easy; wet sections

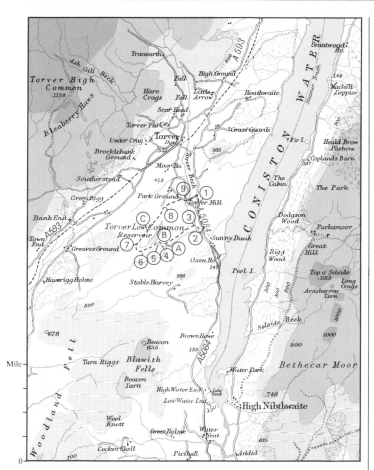

and picnic where you like. The common is managed by the National Park Authority and there is free access.

1 *Park in the loop lay-by opposite the large garage, and walk by roadside down the hill towards Ulverston.*

2 *Path junctions. From the lay-by the one on the left goes to the lake. Take the path opposite and cross the stile.*

3 *Cross the bridge and continue on with the small beck on the left.*

A Note juniper bushes. The local name is 'savins', and the charcoal from it was much used in the manufacture of gunpowder in the district's powder mills. The berries were much valued medicinally for kidney complaints, but of course they are still much used in gin making.

4 *Go right, with the beck, to the tarn.*

B The level of this tarn was raised artificially to maintain a head of water for a mill below.

5 *Walk left along the ridge.*

6 *Cross the wet area at its driest point, that is just before reaching the power lines, then climb hill opposite.*

7 *Walk along the ridge. Small tarn below.*

C Good view over to Coniston Old Man. The crags of Dow are on the left, Goatswater Hause is the dip to the right, and the Old Man is further right again.

8 *Join the path which bears right, to the mill.*

9 *After crossing the mill bridge, go left and through the gate to follow the path to the road. (Join the road with care as it is fairly blind here). Go right to the starting point.*

This is a lazy walk, ideal for a hot summer day when the common here is loud with skylarks, the air heavy with the antiseptic smell of bog myrtle, and the tarn starred with water lilies. Only a few minutes walk from the Torver-Ulverston road can be found an area of remoteness, marred only a little by the skeins of power lines. This is not typical lakeland. Formerly a forest, it is now a stretch of heath and rough grazing for the hardy sheep which feed on myrtle, juniper, and heather shoots as well as grass. The common is largely open and pathless. There are a few crags and no rough ground here. This gives the area a strange sense of freedom; walk where you like, sit

THE BEACON AND BEACON TARN

3¾ miles (6km) 700ft (213.3m) Moderate; some wet sections

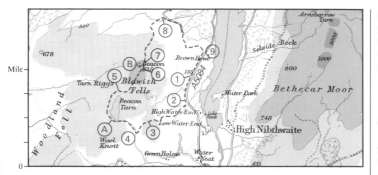

There are beacon points all over Britain and historically they were part of a fairly rapid nation-wide communications system. The sites were chosen so as to be visible from a large area and it should therefore follow that they offer the best viewpoints. The beacon on Blawith Fell overlooking the southern end of Coniston Water is a good example, even though it is of modest height at 835 feet (254.5m). A walk to it would be reward enough, but this route goes by Beacon Tarn, a lovely piece of water which sits below the fell, and this high area is attractive heather moor. Blawith Fell is part of a common in the care of the National Park, so you are free to wander or linger anywhere, but this route is recommended one.

1 *Park at a car parking area on Blawith Common. This is an open area south of Brown Howe on the Torver - Ulverston road, and a mile (1.6km) north of Water Yeat. Walk down the roadside with care, south towards Ulverston.*

2 *After a bend there is an open area with a stream on the right. From here a path can be seen going up the hillside through the bracken. Follow this. It meanders as it climbs and goes between knolls.*

3 *The path descends to a footbridge which can be seen below.*

4 *Cross the footbridge and pick up the path following the beck. Follow it right round the tarn on its western side.*

A Enjoy the quiet tarn. The word 'tarn' has a Norse origin from their word 'tjorn'. Height has only a little to do with why some stretches of water are called tarns and other lakes. Brother's Water (a lake) for instance, is roughly the same height as this tarn. The practised eye can usually tell the difference; there is less luxurious vegetation around a tarn. The Freshwater Biological Association explains the difference between a lake and a tarn in this way. A lake's characteristic emergent plant is the common reed, while in a tarn it is the bottle sedge. In the boggy areas around a tarn two small insectiverous plants can be found. They are the sundew with its round red sticky 'dewy' leaves by which it traps insects and the butterwort, which has broad smooth

sticky leaves lying flat and looks like a small green starfish. The sundew can easily be missed as it merges so well with the moss.

5 *Go right round the top of the tarn to pick up a footpath going up into the fell, Follow this through and along the ridge.*

6 *Just before the path begins a descent take a detour left to Beacon summit.*

B The summit view is mainly eastwards and southwards. Notably one can see the whole length of Coniston Water, surely the best view of the lake from any point. The value as a beacon point can be seen. To the south-west is the hump of Black Combe, the site of another beacon which could take signals and pass them on from as far away as Merseyside and the Isle of Man. Far off to the east the Pennines where there are several beacon points can be seen. One can see over to Morecambe Bay. To the north-east there is Helvellyn on the left and the High Street range on the right. To the north-west the view is dominated by the Coniston Old Man range. Dow Crag, the popular rock-climbing cliff is the high point on the left with the lesser peaks of Buck Pike and Brown Pike to the left again. The central fell is the Old Man and Wetherlam is the body of the fell to the right and behind. Natural little rock gardens on the outcrops, are charming features of this area.

7 *Rejoin the path and start the descent. Several paths join together.*

8 *Join metalled lane and go right.*

9 *Join road and go right to starting point.*

EASEDALE TARN

5 miles (8km) 620ft (188.9m) Moderate; wet underfoot

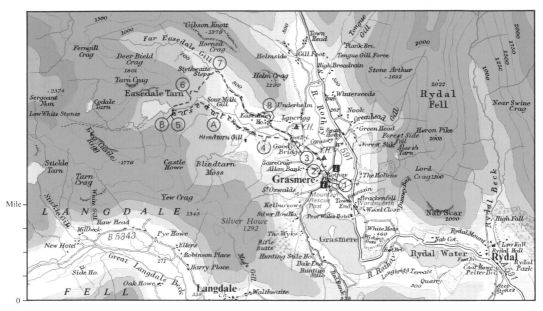

When the Wordsworths lived at Grasmere in the early 19th century they called Easedale 'the black quarter' for that is where the bad weather comes from before it hits the village. Dorothy Wordworth's journal makes several references to their many walks up Easedale, sometimes in search of mosses, but often to enjoy the sight of the waterfall they called 'Churn-milk force' now known as Sour Milk Gill. William, once when in sad mood as he approached the tarn was cheered by the appearance of a rainbow which inspired his small poem, *My Heart Leaps Up* from which these lines are taken.

'My heart leaps up when I behold
A rainbow in the sky'.

Once Dorothy turned back from the walk, frightened when confronted by a cow. Nothing much has changed since then. The falling white water is still a spectacle after heavy rain. The round tarn in its arena of high fells is still a pleasant sight. Perhaps the cows are more placid than they used to be!

This is a favourite short walk from Grasmere marred only by some wet ground which is avoidable, by a wide detour. After heavy rain the stepping-stones at the tarn outlet might be impassable, which would mean a return by the outward route. Strong footwear is essential.

1 *Start the walk in Grasmere village.*
2 *Take the minor road going northwest from the village centre, near the Heaton Cooper studio.*

3 *Turn left when the road reaches the riverside to cross bridges, and follow the good track on.*
4 *Go through the gate and on across the field to another gate and to start the climb.*
A Water cascade. An approach can be made with care.
B Tarn outlet. A good view over the tarn from the high bank.
5 *Cross stepping-stones with care. Follow the path downstream on the opposite bank.*
6 *Boggy ground. The worst can be avoided by a very wide sweep left to the higher ground and back.*
7 *Cross the bridge and follow the path down on the far bank. It changes to a track after a rough descent section.*
8 *Track joins tarmacadam road. Follow this down to join the minor road to starting point.*

THE WORDSWORTH WALK

5 miles (8km) Easy

If Wordsworth only means 'daffodils' then this walk would still be a 'must' among the beautiful and unique gentle landscape of Lake District. If you know a little more about Wordworth and his talented sister Dorothy, and enjoy William's profound philosophy written in some of the finest poetry in the English language, then this walk could take up a very full and memorable day especially if you were to visit *en route*, Dove Cottage, where Wordsworth wrote his best work; the museum alongside and Rydal Mount where Wordsworth lived for the last 37 years of his life. (Dove Cottage is closed on Sunday mornings.)

1 *The walk starts at Grasmere church. Leave the village and go towards main road.*

2 *Cross the road with great care into the road opposite. It is a short distance only to Dove Cottage and museum.*

A Dove cottage was originally a small inn called 'The Dove and Olive Branch'. William and his sister Dorothy rented it as a cottage from December 1799. In 1802 William brought his bride Mary to

the cottage and three children were born to them. They had many visitors including S T Coleridge, Robert Southey and Sir Walter Scott. By 1808 they needed more room and moved from the cottage. It was taken over by Thomas de Quincey whose home it was for 28 years. The museum is next to, but behind the cottage.

3 *Junction, bear left.*

4 *Just past a little tarn the road becomes a track, continue on.*

B A pleasant terraced walk with some old trees and views over Rydal.

5 *At path end turn right down roadway.*

C Rydal Mount. After moving from Dove Cottage the Wordsworths spent five less happy years in unsatisfactory rented accommodation in Grasmere. They moved into Rydal Mount in 1813 and stayed here until William's death in 1850. Wordsworth received hundreds of visitors, many of them distinguished, who had recognised his genius. He was formally acknowledged by his appointment as Poet Laureate in 1843. The garden is laid out to his design.

D Rydal Church. The site was chosen by Wordsworth. Behind it is 'Dora's Field'. Wordsworth planted this with daffodils for the delight of his daughter Dora.

6 *Cross the road and walk short distance towards Grasmere, until footbridge is seen below on the left.*

7 *Cross the footbridge and turn right to follow the river and the banks of Rydal Water.*

8 *Keep with the lakeshore following the clear path.*

E View over Rydal. Nab Cottage opposite. De Quincey lodged here and then married the landlord's daughter, taking her to Dove Cottage. Wordsworth did not approve. The house was later the home of Hartley Coleridge, the great poet's son.

9 *Go through the small gateway right and descend through the wood to the river.*

10 *Do not cross footbridge but go left on the river bank to Grasmere's outlet.*

F Good view over Grasmere. Helm Crag is in the distance.

11 *Path junction at wall. Keep with lakeshore path.*

12 *Path on shore ends at a boat house and fence and turns upwards towards the road.*

13 *Join the road and descend with it in to Grasmere village.*

14 *Go into the churchyard behind the church.*

G William Wordsworth and his wife Mary are buried under simple stones by the river. Dora, William's favourite daughter, whose married name was Quillinan is in the next grave.

ELTERWATER AND THE WATERFALLS

4½ miles (6.8km) Moderate; some mud after rain

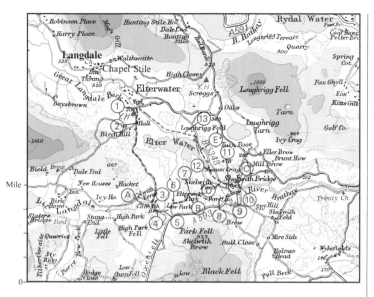

'Elter' is old Norse for 'swan'. So this is swan lake and aptly named for it is one place visited by Whooper Swans fleeing from their Siberian winter. It is a strangely-shaped little lake fed unusually in its middle reaches at opposite sides by the river Brathay from Little Langdale in the south, and by Great Langdale Beck in the north. Its banks are reedy, unapproachable, and subject to flooding, but there is some valuable grazing land. Therefore on much of the walk described, one has to be content with an aggravatingly distant view, but there are compensations. The view from the lakeside path on the south-west, with the Pikes in the background is a classic, and there are two waterfalls, one with an awkward approach, but the other is very close. Needless to say these are at their best after prolonged rain, when some sections of this walk are muddy.

1 *The walk starts at the bridge in Elterwater village. If the car park here is full there is a car park on the common to the north of the village. Walk south from the bridge towards Little Langdale.*

2 *Continue past the Hotel, on a metalled minor road.*

3 *Road junction, go left and across the bridge.*

4 *Detour right, over the stile on to National Trust land and on to the falls.*

A This pretty fall is about 46ft (14m). The Brathay rises on Wrynose Pass. Until Local Government reorganisation in 1974 it was the boundary between Westmorland to the north, and Lancashire in the south.

5 *Having retraced steps, cross the stile*

on the opposite side of the road and take the path which starts on a field then climbs steeply up the wooded bank and into another field.

6 *Keep to right of farmhouse, up steps and through the stile.*

B Notice practice (or sample ?) lettering on stone in barn wall.

7 *Go through farmyard, and walk on track bearing right.*

8 *Do not go on the track to road, but continue on to the wood.*

9 *Path goes in front of cottages then joins road; go left.*

10 *After crossing the bridge, go left by the riverside to the slate quarry yard.*

C Showrooms of slate quarry. The slate is formed from volcanic dust laid down in water millions of years ago. It was then subject to enormous pressures. The 'ripple' effect in some of the slate shows well especially when the slate has been sawed and polished. The slate is sawn here with circular saws set with diamond cutters. The slate is much sought after, all over the world and is very often used to face prestigious buildings. Do not assume that slate lying around here is waste.

11 *Continue on to falls.*

D Skelwith Force is not high, but through this narrow gap flows all the water from Great and Little Langdale. 'Force' is certainly the right word.

12 *Continue on the riverside path through the fields.*

E A classic viewpoint over the reeds and water to Langdale Pikes.

13 *At the end of the wood go on riverside path (National Trust property) to starting point.*

TROUTBECK AND WANSFELL PIKE FROM AMBLESIDE

6 miles (9.7km) Strenuous

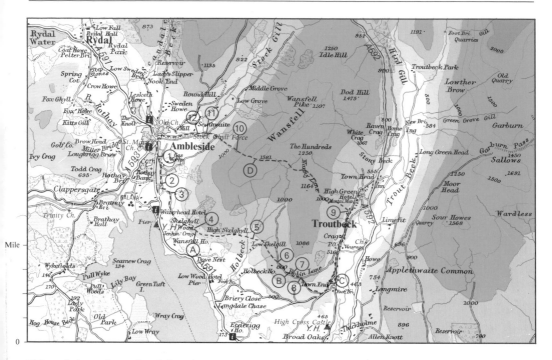

This walk has a feast of varied attractions. It offers some of the best viewpoints over the northern reaches of Windermere and to the central fells. It is a walk through a renowned and unspoilt 17th century village (with a chance to look inside one of the houses owned by the National Trust); a walk up to another viewpoint at an airy 1500ft (457.2m) with a very wide panoramic view and as a grand finale, particularly after heavy rain, a look at one of the best known waterfalls. All this cannot be achieved without encountering a few snags such as wet sections of path, a steady climb up a low fell and a steep descent. The walk should be done in clear weather. Some people might find the thought of a climb rather daunting but anyone who is reasonably fit should be able to cope, especially if the walk is taken at a leisurely pace. A visit to Town End, the house owned by The National Trust and open to the public, is well worthwhile. Take a picnic lunch and make a day of it.

1 *Park in Ambleside and walk south towards Windermere from the town centre. Take the old Lake Road left from the main road.*

2 *Go left upwards on a narrow tarmac lane.*

3 *Keep right on the contour with views and enter the woodland.*

4 *Look for The National Trust sign on the right ('Jenkin Crag') and divert on the path to the viewpoint.*

A A viewpoint from a craggy spur with superb views over the lake to the central fells.

5 *After crossing the bridge turn upwards from the well-defined way through a field.*

6 *Join Robin Lane.*

7 *Look for the stone cairn up in the field on the left. Walk up to it.*

B Another spectacular viewpoint.

8 *Go down the lane on the right to join the road and go left.*

C Town End; the 17th century house open to the public. Go into the village. Note the 'bank barn'

Over

opposite Town End. This barn design is a typical old Lake District one. Hay is taken in at the high floor level and fed to the cattle which enter at the 'ground floor' below. This type of barn is typical of those found in Scandinavia, thus giving further credence to the belief that there was extensive Viking settlement in ancient times in the Lake District. Walk on through the village and note the interesting architectural features. The buildings are all built from stone slate, quarried locally. The oldest are 17th century but there was further building during the more prosperous period of the 18th and 19th centuries. The large cylindrical chimneys are tradi-

tional in the district. The village is really a succession of hamlets, each grouped round the communal wells, which are named after saints; St John, St James, St Margaret. Unusually, the church is hidden away outside and below the village. This was because it had to serve several settlements scattered all over the valley.

9 *After St Margaret's Well watch for the signed path going left from a barn end for Wansfell Pike, but divert first along the road if you wish to see an interesting old sign at the Mortal Man. Walk up Nanny Lane, looking backwards at the valley views, to the fell path leaving left for Wansfell Pike.*

D Here, there are views which open out suddenly as you climb. If it is clear there is a splendid panoramic view over all the main fells from Coniston Old Man on the left to the High Street range on the right. The highest land, including Scafell, Scafell Pike, Great Gable and Bowfell can be seen a little north of west.

10 **Descend slowly with great care** *to the lane and turn left.*

11 *Watch for the gate into a wooded ravine containing Stock Ghyll waterfalls.*

E There are several falls, the main one of which is 60ft (18.3m).

12 *Follow the path down by the ghyll side to Ambleside.*

53

ROUND LOUGHRIGG

6 miles (9.7km) Easy; wet patches

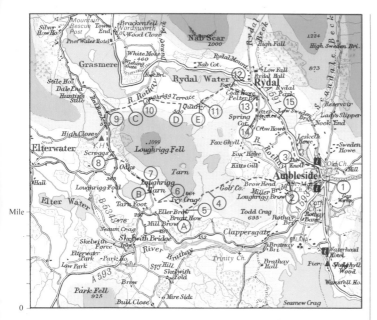

In the central Lake District is the essence of the National Park's peaceful landscape; the view over the head of Windermere; the view over Elterwater to Coniston fells, Langdale and the Pikes from Loughrigg Tarn; over Grasmere to Helm Crag and Dunmail, and over Rydal Water to Fairfield. All this can be seen on one walk circumnavigating Loughrigg Fell, a sort of natural grandstand for the large and glorious free show. Loughrigg Terrace is famous for its high level view and yet it is not a strenuous climb. For good measure the walk goes near the huge man-made cave in the old quarry on the north side of the fell.

1 Start the walk at Ambleside church.

Go past the churchyard, through the iron gate at the end and into the parkland. Follow path to Miller Bridge.

2 Cross the bridge and turn right on the minor road. Walk for a short distance and just beyond the cattle grid go left.

3 Follow surfaced lane, going right at the end of buildings where it becomes a rough track. Follow this past the old golf club house.

4 A number of paths here. Go left with the beck.

5 Path junction. Go right.

A Viewpoint. Particularly west over Elterwater towards Coniston Old Man range.

6 As the path descends, watch for the short cut footpath on the right.

7 Join the lane, to follow it right.

B Viewpoint up Langdale to the Pikes over the delightful Loughrigg Tarn.

8 Lane joins minor road. Turn right and continue to beyond road junction.

9 Watch for turning right, descending on track into trees. Follow this track on, ignoring the left-hand turn.

C Loughrigg Terrace. A grand view over Grasmere, Helm Crag ('The Lion and the Lamb') behind.

10 Path junction. Take the path going right at a higher level.

D View over Rydal Water, Nab Scar, a spur of the Fairfield range behind.

E The Rydal Caves. These were once profitable quarry holes. The slate was of fine quality. The slates here were formed from very fine volcanic ash laid down in shallow seas millions of years ago. The beds of the best kind vary in thickness between 10 and 120ft (3-36.6m). Here it was easier to cut into the beds rather than open them out from the surface. Some of this slate has an attractive 'ripple' effect in its colouration, making it particularly suitable for decorative facing.

11 Descend on old quarry track towards Rydal Water.

12 Bear right through the gate and go along lane.

13 Turn right at the bridge to continue on a surfaced minor road.

14 Stepping-stones left. Cross these and walk onwards up footpath across field to road. (**NB:** If the river level is high making crossing the stepping-stones tricky, dangerous, or impossible, continue on down this minor road which will bring you to Miller Bridge and the start of the walk).

15 Road. Turn right for Ambleside.

GLEN MARY, TARN HOWS AND TOM HEIGHTS

3 miles (4.8km) 700ft (213.3m) Some steep sections; moderate

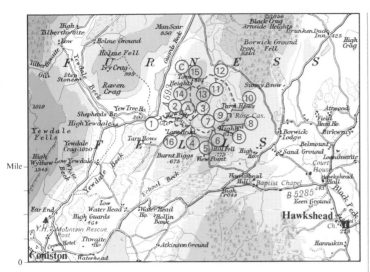

10 *Junction. Continue on the main path.*

11 *Junction of three paths. (Main one ascends steeply ahead). Take the right-hand path over the stile.*

12 *After a second stile go left up the bank on narrow path through the bracken. It gets more distinct ahead.*

13 *Just before the path begins its descent go right on a less plain path going up the fell.*

14 *Reach the ridge and go right for summit cairn.*

C There are glorious views from all points on this ridge to Coniston Water, through the high fells to Helvellyn and across to Windermere. This is a place to linger. The extraordinary variety of scenery here occurs because this point is in a geological complex. This is the junction between the Borrowdale Volcanic series which characterises the high fells, and the Silurian slates landscape which is lush with woodlands and without the harsh crags. Examples of Silurian slate lie south, and east of Coniston Water. In between is the narrow band of Coniston limestone, a grey limestone which geologists might have spotted *en route.*

15 *From the summit go south along the ridge to the end to pick up one of the paths descending left to the tarn near the dam. Pick up the track by the tarn and cross the dam again. Ascend the hill and watch right for the stone track descending right.*

16 *Follow this track which changes to a pleasant grassy terraced path. Go all the way down to join the road (close the gates). Go right for the starting point.*

Tarn Hows is a famous beauty spot and with little wonder. The subtle blend of varied ingredients: mixed woodland, calm water against a magnificent backcloth of hills has a magic quality which cannot fail to captivate. Alas the atmosphere is sometimes spoiled by the crowds on good summer weekends when the car parks are jammed. This is a walk-in route however. Its surprises are the little dell pretentiously named a 'glen' and the exhilarating view from Tom Heights. The best time for the walk is on a clear mid-week day.

1 *Park in one of the lay-bys just south of the little tarn on the roadside between Coniston (2 miles/3.2km) and Skelwith Bridge (3 miles/4.8km) Commence the walk on the **north** side of the gill.*

2 *There are several paths. Keep close to the gill so that you do not miss the waterfalls. Follow the path all the way.*

A *A lovely little waterfall in an intimate verdant setting.*

3 *Join the track near the dam. Turn right to cross dam and follow the track round the tarn.*

4 *Do not go right up to the road but continue as if going round the tarn.*

5 *Approach the kissing-gate. Look up to see the little summit crowned by a standing stone. This is the next objective but not directly.*

6 *Go through the kissing-gate then turn **right** up the path.*

7 *Leave path for a feinter one, going left to viewpoint.*

B *One of the best views of the tarn. The stone records the names of the donors, Sir James and Lady Scott, who gave Tarn Hows to The National Trust in 1930.*

8 *From viewpoint go right to join the track.*

9 *Junction. Descend left.*

TARN HOWS FROM HAWKSHEAD

6 miles (9.7km) 500ft (152.4m) Moderate

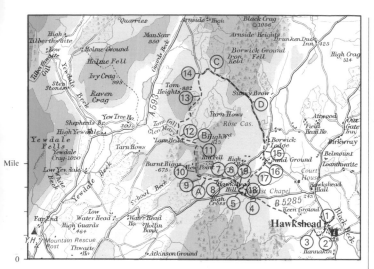

Tarn Hows is visited by thousands of people each year. It is the best known beauty spot in the Lake District and indeed one of the best known in Britain. Some people prefer to steer clear of the popular, but Tarn Hows cannot be ignored. It is a jewel of a tarn with little promontories and islands all set among a happy mixture of trees, hardwoods and conifers, with the spectacular backdrop of Langdale Fells. It is a perfectly balanced scene, best viewed in early spring in its many shades of green; or in the autumn's blaze. It can be marred only perhaps on hot days when too many people congregate around the water's edge and so break up the picture's foreground. In high summer, for this reason, it is best enjoyed in the early morning or late evening. This walk goes all the way from Hawkshead, returning by what is known as 'the mountain road'.

1 *The start is at Hawkshead church. Walk through the churchyard and on to path beyond.*

2 *Take the path bearing right to join a minor road.*

3 *Cross the minor road and take the path, signposted, across the fields.*

4 *Join the road, turn left up it.*

5 *Turn right at the first junction.*

6 *Cross the road and go up the one signposted Tarn Hows.*

7 *Look for a stile over the wall on the left. Cross it and go on with the wall for a short distance, then over another stile and continue.*

8 *Walk across to the wall corner, take the stile which goes over into wood (not the one straight on).*

A *A most pleasant wood to begin as it has a mixture of trees. Further on the trees are mainly larch. All this area is in the care of The National Trust.*

9 *Walk on through the wood to a path junction close to a minor road.*

10 *Do **not** join road but go left before it to follow the wall on a path which runs parallel to the road.*

11 *Join the road at the hill top and walk on the left overlooking the tarn.*

B *There are many viewpoints here. Take your choice!*

12 *Descend to the dam wall and follow the main path going from it.*

13 *Watch for a turn left to leave the tarn. It is approached after rising and descending on a rocky portion of path, and just as the tarn is seen close ahead. Cross the stile and go forward on a pleasant walk through open woodland.*

14 *Join a rough, unmetalled road. Go up to the right.*

C *Viewpoint near crest of hill. Left for unusual view of Langdale Pikes. On the extreme left but closer is Wetherlam.*

D *View of Ambleside left over the gate. Esthwaite Water ahead.*

15 *Join the road and go down the minor road almost immediately opposite.*

16 *After passing buildings and crossing a little bridge go right (signed) across a field. The path is obscure here. Aim for a point to the right of the wooded knoll ahead.*

17 *Pinch stile ('fatman's agony') in the wall. Go through this and on with wall on the left, go on the same line.*

18 *Go through the gate, bear right and through another gate, and on over a cattle bridge right of the buildings to a gate opposite a telephone box and on to the road.*

19 *Turn left and retrace to Hawkshead.*

Walk 36
LATTERBARROW
5 miles (8km) 570ft (173.7m) Moderate; some steep and boggy sections

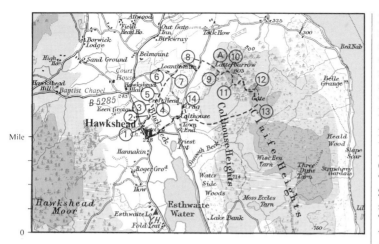

Blisco nearer and right. Behind then is Bowfell 2960ft (902.2m). The main part of the Scafell Pike mass is obscured except for Great End the most northerly point. Further right are Allen Crags and Glaramara, and then the unmistakeable Langdale Pikes with the crag face of Pavey Ark. Then there are the fells of High White Stones, Ullscarf and Armboth by Thirlmere with the Grasmere fells in front. Well behind Thirlmere, if conditions are right, Skiddaw, 3054ft (930.8m) can be seen some 19 miles (30.5km) away. Then, nearer, the Helvellyn range with Dollywaggon Pike, the nearest peak. Nearer still is the Fairfield range, due north, and Kirkstone Pass, the highest road pass at 1476ft (449.8m). The spot of white is an inn. The High Street range is further right still. East are the Pennines; south is Morecambe Bay. However, to see the Ambleside end of Windermere it is necessary to walk a short distance to the east.

10 *From the summit go south directly down the path parallel with a forest fence to a stile.*

11 *Go over it and follow the path through forest left.*

12 *Go right here for a short distance and then a wall gap on the left will be seen. Go through this and descend the steep steps with care to pick up a path going by a fence and broken wall to a T-junction and a gateway.*

13 *Go right on the track all the way avoiding the less clear detours. Muddy sections can normally be avoided with care.*

14 *Join the road and follow it left to Hawkshead.*

Visitors to Hawkshead are often intrigued by the summit to the north-east which is crowned by a tall column of a cairn. This is Latterbarrow. Some set off to investigate, though the routes to it are by no means plain. The views from the summit justify the effort in reaching it. The walk back through forest is very pleasant. There can be some very muddy sections after prolonged rain, when this should be regarded as a 'wellies' walk, (so long as care is taken on the steep descents).

1 *Starting at Hawkshead village centre go down the alleyway alongside the Red Lion. Cross the road and continue on to a footbridge.*

2 *Go left after the bridge then bear right to a kissing gate.*

3 *Bear right across a field over a sleeper bridge to a stile.*

4 *Go left to the next stile which is at a wall end and continue to the wicket gate to join the surfaced lane.*

5 *Go left for 50 yards (46m) then go through the stile on the right under the oak tree. Follow a fence on the right, for a short distance to another stile by a gate.*

6 *Follow the hedge at first, then go right to a stile by a gate. To right of farm there is a step-stile onto a minor road. Aim for this.*

7 *Go right at the minor road to T-junction. Go left.*

8 *Walk through the gate (signed) and on up the path.*

9 *Turn left and up the hill by any of the paths to the summit cairn.*

A The view is surprisingly extensive. This proves that the best viewpoints are not necessarily the highest ones. Hawkshead is far below. Behind is Grizedale Forest and beyond that, to the west, the Coniston Old Man range with its nearest arm, Wetherlam, looming large on the right. Next are the 'crinkles' of Crinkle Crags, Pike o'

CLAIFE HEIGHTS WOODLANDS AND LAKESHORE WALK

7¾ miles (12.5km) 830ft (252.9m) Strenuous; some rough and steep sections

William Wordsworth was critical of the rich people who had discovered the Lake District in his time and were buying lakeshore land and building extravagant mansions unsympathetic to the delicate landscape. Many, he thought, were lacking in taste, such as the round building on Belle Isle in Windermere, built by a Mr English in 1774. Wordsworth called it a 'pepper-pot'. It was bought by Mrs Curwen of Workington Hall seven years later and her husband, John Christian Curwen, was a great tree planter. Not only did he landscape and plant up Belle Isle, but also much of the Windermere west shore woodlands north of the ferry were his inspiration. Windermere's beauty owes so much to him. This is a lakeshore and woodland walk for tree enthusiasts. Some of the land is under Forestry Commission plantations, but even here the otherwise boring lines of conifers are broken up with groups of hardwoods.

If walkers dislike noise this walk should not be done at fine weekends when there is a lot of lake activity.

Over

1 *Start the walk at Bowness and walk to the ferry road.*

2 *Cross on ferry.*

3 *Disembark and walk between the buildings.*

4 *Take the short cut on the right of way by the lakeshore to join the lakeshore. Continue on this road.*

5 *Keep to the lakeshore. After a while the road is unsurfaced.*

6 *The road leaves the lakeside for a short distance to go round a caravan site.*

A Watch for some fine tree specimens, notably some tall straight Douglas Fir between the road and the lake.

7 *A wall and a boathouse are reached. Here track goes left upwards with the wall, signposted 'Bridlepath to Hawkshead'. The way is very rough, and quite steep.*

B It is now probably hard to believe but this was once a horse-and-carriage road to Hawkshead from the Windermere ferry which used to ply from Miller Ground opposite. Part of the old paving can be seen near the top.

8 *Junction of paths. Continue on 'hollow' path which now bears right.*

C Conifer plantations are broken by hardwoods. There are many deer in these woods, watch for signs; biting and stripping of bark by red deer; barking of small saplings by roebucks 'fraying' with their antlers to mark their territory; small mishapen trees which have been damaged by deer browsing; tracks in the soft ground. If the woods are quiet the sharp-sighted have a chance of seeing deer.

9 *Care is needed here. A forest road is reached. Cross the road and almost immediately afterwards there is a Y-junction. The way right is the continuation of the bridleway to Hawkshead. Our route is left up a path overhung by trees.*

10 *A forest road is reached. Cross it to join a path going straight ahead. This joins the forest track higher up, and eventually leaves the forest at a gate.*

11 *After the gate follow the wall to the right. This is a boggy section. It can be avoided by a detour left or right. A green path continues.*

12 *Two pieces of water are approached, Wise Een Tarn right (on private land), and a fish pond left. To avoid a very boggy section walk close to fish pond's dam. After this, the path becomes more clear as it goes through a gate and nears Moss Eccles Tarn.*

D Classic viewpoint over tarn towards Langdale Pikes.

E Moss Eccles Tarn is in the care of The National Trust. A pleasant place to sit and rest.

13 *Continue on the track now, and keep left.*

14 *Watch for the left turn at Y-junction. (Signed 'Bridleway Far Sawrey')*

15 *Join the road and go left through the hamlet.*

16 *After Sawrey Hotel go left up a track.*

17 *At the junction, keep right.*

18 *Another junction, keep right again. Eventually the path descends through woodland.*

19 *Watch for the short cut which goes right through a gate towards the lakeside road visible below. Take this to the road.*

WINDERMERE SHORE WALK TO LAKESIDE
7 miles (11.3km) Easy; not passable when lake is at abnormally high level

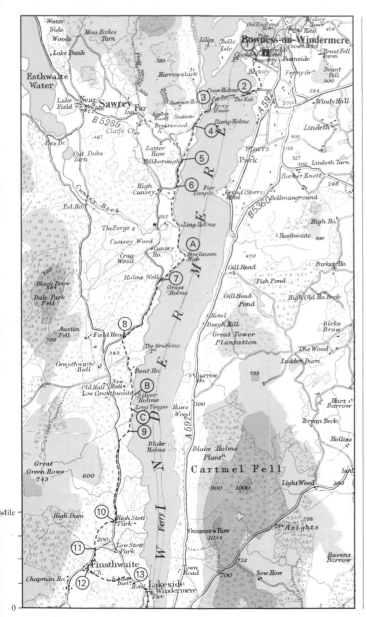

Windermere lakeshore south of the ferry on the western side has a good public footpath which makes a pleasant seven miles (11.3km) walk, marred only by two miles (3.2km) of walking on minor roads which can be busy at holiday times. Those who like quietness will avoid the walk at summer weekends when the lake is noisy with motor boats. This is not a 'round' walk and the return trip will need to be done by service boat from Lakeside. Collect a timetable before starting and study it. Allow at least three hours for the walk, longer if you have slow walkers or wish to stop for refreshment or photography. An alternative finish would be to take the steam train on the private line from Lakeside to Haverthwaite and bus back to Bowness, the starting point. Again study the timetables before setting out. The walker must cross the lake by ferry which leaves every twenty minutes, and more frequently in high season.

1 *The walk starts at the southern end of Bowness promenade where the road crooks beyond the car park. In the corner is an iron gate which leads to the lakeshore path. (Cockshot Point) The path eventually leads to the road and to the ferry.*

2 *Board the ferry.*

3 *Walk along the road towards Hawkshead. A dangerous corner can be avoided by going into the wood on the right. There is a pleasant viewpoint on a crag above the road.*

4 *Rejoin the road then go left on a track by the lakeshore.*

5 *Join the minor road and go left.*

6 *A path leaves the road by the bend, and goes to the lakeshore. Continue.*

A Viewpoint. Up the lake is a view as far as Belle Isle which appears to be the lake end. Down the lake there are attractive woodlands.

7 *The path rejoins minor road. Go left.*

8 *The path leaves the road beyond the brow of the hill, and goes down to the shore through the trees.*

B Silver Holme is the small island opposite, on which it was believed there was a silver horde hidden.

C Good viewpoint.

9 *Path leaves the shore by a fence and wall. Join the road. Some pleasanter walking away from the traffic can be had by ascending the bank on the right.*

10 *The road to Lakeside pier is dangerous beyond this point and this detour is recommended. Take the lane on the right after the buildings.*

Bear left at the fork and go through the gate and across a field. The path goes towards a point where two walls converge, and reaches a minor road eventually.

11 *Turn right and go into Finsthwaite village.*

12 *Turn left and go past a church and school on to a footpath along a field and through the wood to the road.*

13 *Turn right for short walk to Lakeside pier.*

UNDERBARROW AND CUNSWICK SCARS

7 miles (11.3km) 625ft (190.5m) Moderate; some steepness

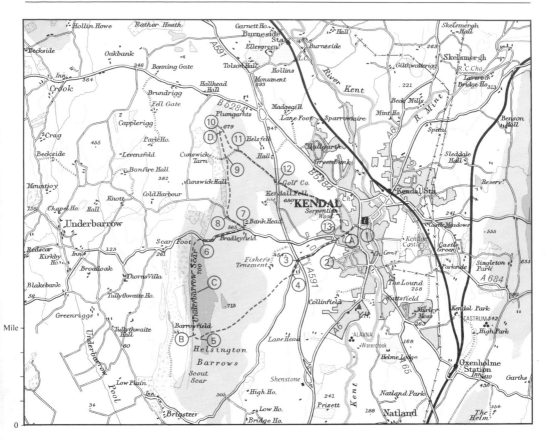

The main appeal of this walk from Kendal is the view on a clear day which bursts as a visual bombshell as the edge of a limestone precipice is reached. Given the right conditions the whole of the Lake District's central fells are revealed across a lovely green valley far below, with pastures, woodland and hedges, hamlets and farmsteads. No skilful town and country planners laid out this landscape. It evolved naturally. But the walk is also one

for the naturalist, as the ridges of carboniferous limestone, with 'pavements' have the rich distinctive flora. The walk begins by going through a Kendal suburb, which is quiet and pleasant.

1 *Start at Kendal Town Hall. Walk up All Hallows Lane opposite.*

A The obelisk on the left is on the site of what was Kendal's Norman motte and bailey castle, built in the 11th century and replaced a century later by the castle on the east of the

town. The obelisk also commemorates the revolution of 1688.

2 *Road junctions. The one on the left goes to the hospital. Take the middle road - Brigsteer Road.*

3 *The road crosses the bridge.*

4 *After passing some stone gateposts on the right seek a stile there (signposted). Cross it and pick up the grassy path across a meadow, through the iron gate in the wall, and on to another stile and straight on.*

Over

B The view to the far fells includes, looking left to right, the Coniston Old Man range some 13 miles (21km) away as the crow flies; Langdale Pikes some 17 miles (27km) distant. Beyond them, the roof of England with Scafell Pike (3210ft/978m) about 20 miles (32km) away. Then there are the fells of Grasmere, Fairfield and Helvellyn (17 miles/27km) before reaching the High Street range. On the extreme left is a view across Morecambe Bay.

5 *The edge of escarpment. Go right and follow the path on the cliff edge*

C Eccentric monstrosity is the 'mushroom' which once served as an indicator for the view. On the cliff edge discerning botanists will note that the Whitebeam here is *Sorbus Aria var rupicola* a variety which grows here, in Scotland and Scandinavia.

6 *The path joins the road by the kissing-gate. Go right alongside the road.*

7 *Watch for a signed track starting on the left before the house. Go left up it.*

8 *Do* **not** *go through gate, but turn right just before it to pick up a path going round the wall corner and alongside a walled wood.*

9 *Follow the path on the edge of the escarpment to the cairned summit.*

D Main interest apart from the flora is the view north and north-west.

10 *The path doubles back at a sharp angle. It is not distinct at first on the grass but is more visible further on when it aims for the footbridge over the bypass road.*

11 *There is a stile at the corner. Continue on from it.*

12 *The path continues over the footbridge and goes in a fairly straight line on through stiles ('fatman's agonies'). The path is a little obscured by the golf course mowing but goes on the same line, then bears to the left-hand corner of a large wood.*

13 *From a viewpoint with seats there is a commanding prospect of the town. Join the paths meandering through Serpentine Woods. Eventually any one of them leads to a road and down into Kendal centre.*

ORREST HEAD WALK

2½ miles (4km) Moderate; some wet patches

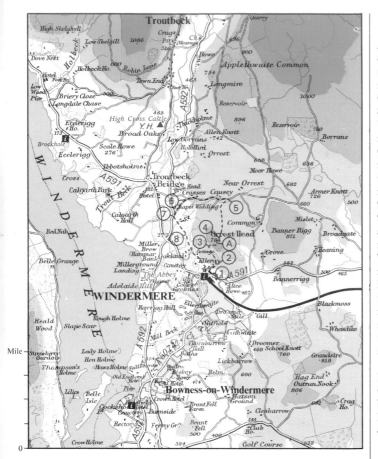

then go through an iron gate at the end and up to the viewpoint.

A There is a plinth with a view indicator, sometimes alas unreadable through vandalism. Directly and more prominently in front is the Coniston Old Man range (2631ft/801.9m) with the bulky shoulder of Wetherlam to the right. Further right are the humps of Crinkle Crags with Pike O'Blisco in the foreground. Beyond, continuing to the right, is the Scafell range, with its highest point Scafell Pike (3210ft/978m); nearer is Bowfell (2960ft/902.2m) and Esk Pike to the right again. Beyond is Great End, the northern hump of the Scafell range. The Pikes of Langdale are readily recognisable, as are the ridges of High Raise and Ullscarf. Look to the north-west and see the Fairfield range, with Wansfell, above Ambleside in front. To the north-east is the High Street range. Further east are the Yorkshire Hills.

There is an excellent view of the lake, with the woodland facing Claife Heights. The lake appears to be shorter than it is as Belle Isle looks like a southern shoreline.

4 *Walk on north on a path from the summit. This crosses fields towards a distant roadway. Wet areas can be avoided with care.*

5 *Cross the stile on to a minor road. Turn left down it.*

6 *Keep left on a surfaced road. Join the major road and turn left to walk a short distance.*

7 *Go through the iron gate on to a track.*

8 *Follow the track and path to starting point.*

Orrest Head is a short walk from Windermere Town, yet it is one of the most rewarding viewpoints in the district, giving an astonishing panorama of the central mountains. It is best done on a clear day. The walk goes beyond the Head across the fields and back through the woods of Elleray Bank.

1 *The walk starts from the north side of* the A591 almost opposite to its junction with the road down to Bowness and the railway station approach. It begins up a tarmacadam lane.

2 *Follow the tarmacadam lane as far as it goes. It turns into an unsurfaced track to a terrace with a seat (good viewpoint for the lake) then into a path going over tree roots by a wall.*

3 *A track is reached, go right with it,*